FEEDING THE EMPTY HEART

Feeding the Empty Heart

Adult Children and Compulsive Eating

Barbara McFarland and Tyeis Baker-Baumann

1817

A Harper/Hazelden Book
Harper & Row, Publishers, San Francisco
Cambridge, Hagerstown, New York, Philadelphia, Washington
London, Mexico City, São Paulo, Singapore, Sydney

First Harper & Row edition published in 1988.

Library of Congress Cataloging-in-Publication Data

McFarland, Barbara.
    Feeding the empty heart.

    "A Harper/Hazelden book."
    1. Compulsive eating.   2. Adult children of
alcoholics.   3. Co-dependence (Psychology)   I. Baker-
Baumann, Tyeis.   II. Title.
RC552.C65M25   1988   616.85′2   87-46216
ISBN 0-06-255483-2

  89   90   91   92   Haz   10   9   8   7   6   5   4

With appreciation to Harold and Bill and especially to all of the women we have worked with.

CONTENTS

INTRODUCTION

Are You a Compulsive Eater?

	YES	NO
1. Do you eat when you're not hungry?	____	____
2. Do you go on eating binges for no apparent reason?	____	____
3. Do you have feelings of guilt and remorse after overeating?	____	____
4. Do you give too much time and thought to food?	____	____
5. Do you look forward with pleasure and anticipation to the moments when you can eat alone?	____	____
6. Do you plan secret binges ahead of time?	____	____
7. Do you eat sensibly with others, but not alone?	____	____
8. Is your weight affecting the way you live your life?	____	____
9. Have you tried to diet for a week (or longer), only to fall short of your goal?	____	____
10. Do you resent the advice of others who tell you to "use a little willpower" to stop overeating?	____	____
11. Despite evidence to the contrary, have you continued to assert you can diet on your own whenever you wish?	____	____
12. Do you crave to eat at a definite time, day or night, other than at mealtime?	____	____
13. Do you eat to escape from worries or troubles?	____	____
14. Has your physician ever treated you for being overweight?	____	____
15. Does your food obsession make you unhappy?	____	____

If you check "yes" to three or more of these questions you may be a compulsive eater.

For the past five years, we have been treating individuals who suffer from the addictive illness of compulsive eating. In writing this book we use the term *compulsive eater*. Many people compulsively eat from time to time, but compulsive eaters are out of control with food on a daily basis. Their quality of life is often affected by their relationship with food. Their eating disorder becomes part of their sense of *self*.

Compulsive eaters suffer from a hidden disease that is chronic and progressive. It not only has physical consequences, such as hypertension and cardiovascular problems, but also affects the self-esteem of its victims. It ravages a person inside, while others may not be aware of what is happening. More media attention is being given to eating disorders, especially anorexia and bulimia.

Compulsive undereaters starve themselves and are clinically referred to as anorexics. *Anorexics* are obsessed with not eating and may have an unnatural fear of food. They may be repulsed by their bodies and see themselves as heavier than they really are. Anorexics try to feel they are in control of their bodies.

A person who is *bulimic* binges by secretly eating large amounts of foods in a brief time. Bingeing may be followed by restrictive dieting, vomiting, abusing laxatives or diuretics (increasing the flow of urine), or taking medications that induce vomiting. We are not addressing Adult Children of Alcoholics (ACOA) issues related to anorexia nervosa. In this book, we are only addressing ACOAs who are compulsive eaters. We define compulsive eaters as people who are clinically referred to as bulimic and people who may be overweight. Not all overweight people are compulsive eaters, but many of them are.

Obesity has always been recognized as a problem but has been viewed as a self-control issue rather than an illness. In our culture, which prizes being thin and fit, the overweight person is looked on with disdain—stigmatized as not being in control. Being in control is important to many Americans.

We have often heard our overweight patients say they wish they could be anorexic or bulimic, believing then they would look normal. Measuring up to the ideal body image seems more important to them than the self-destructive behaviors of anorexics or bulimics, like starving and vomiting.

Compulsive over- or undereaters have an unhealthy relationship with food. They are driven by an obsession to be thin. To the compulsive eater, thinness symbolizes power and control. They believe they can achieve these through their body size.

In our experience, we have become aware that many of our patients are codependents, with the vast majority being ACOAs. In working with these individuals we have asked ourselves, what is it that makes ACOAs more likely to eat compulsively? Although not all compulsive eaters come from an alcoholic family, a common thread is that ACOAs who are compulsive eaters are products of a codependent family system. We accept the definition of *codependency* Melody Beattie uses in her book *Codependent No More*:

> A person who has let someone else's behavior affect him or her and is obsessed with controlling other people's behavior.

A codependent family system is a dysfunctional, non-equal relationship between spouses, who both may have low self-esteem. Spouses look to others to get needs met, often without knowing what their needs are and without directly discussing their needs. Since they're unable to meet their own needs they're unable to meet the needs of their children.

Children who grow up in families where one or both parents are alcoholic are especially prone to developing an eating disorder. In this book, we have outlined what we believe are major contributors to ACOAs developing an eating disorder.

We have presented our material from what we consider to be a stereotypical family with an alcohol problem: the father as alcoholic, the mother as chief *enabler* (she takes on more and more of the alcoholic's responsibilities as his drinking continues), and a daughter who is the child most likely to develop an eating disorder. We have done this for three reasons:

1. This book is based on our clinical experience with ACOAs who are compulsive eaters. Most of our patients who are compulsive eaters are women who had an alcoholic father and enabling mother.
2. Sex role conflicts play an important part in the development of an eating disorder and are easiest to understand within the framework of a stereotypical alcoholic family system.
3. Statistically, eating disorders afflict women more often than men. More is known about female compulsive eaters because they are more likely to seek help, whereas men are given the cultural message that men should be strong and be able to solve their own problems. Women experience cultural pressures that emphasize the way they should look. Because society's idea that body image and weight may dictate a woman's femininity, women are more susceptible to eating disorders.

Once the concepts of male-female sex roles and the roles of alcoholics and enablers are understood, these concepts can be applied to a variety of family situations: mother as alcoholic and father as enabler; stepparents, friends, relatives, or grandparents as either alcoholics or enablers. The intensity and connection between certain developmental issues, how a family interacts, parents' sex role orientations, and social and cultural pressures may make a person more likely to develop an eating disorder.

Chapter One presents an overview of the alcoholic family system and the roles family members play. We will summarize the most recent information about ACOAs.

Chapter Two presents an overview of compulsive eating as an addictive illness. It focuses on the family and social and cultural factors that contribute to an eating disorder. This chapter will familiarize the reader with compulsive eating as a disease, the most common family dynamics, and the personality traits of the compulsive eater.

Chapter Three discusses the relationship between ACOA issues and compulsive eating. We discuss each of the following factors that we feel contributes to an eating disorder in an alcoholic family system.

1. The child's emotional development and the severity of the alcoholism in the family.
2. The parents' acceptance of typical sexual roles and rigid adherence to stereotypical sex-appropriate behaviors and attitudes.
3. The family's value on food and weight.
4. The child's level of emotional involvement in the family system.

Chapter Four discusses effective treatment options and outlines recovery for the ACOA who is a compulsive eater.

Chapter Five presents a series of personal stories of adult children and their struggle with compulsive eating. The individual stories are composites of patients we have worked with. We have not used their real names, and we have in all cases disguised other clues to their identities. In gathering these stories, we have highlighted what we feel are the most common struggles for the ACOA who is a compulsive eater.

We have chosen to use the feminine third person pronoun throughout this text. This is not intended to exclude men or to indicate they do not suffer from this illness. Due to cultural influences, women tend to suffer from this illness in greater numbers. Our clinical experience has been primarily with females.

We hope this book increases your understanding of the ACOA and compulsive eating.

CHAPTER
- 1 -

Adult Children of Alcoholics and the Alcoholic Family System

Only recently has attention been given to individuals who grew up in an alcoholic family. Prior to the 1980s, treatment focused on the alcoholic. It was assumed that if the alcoholism could be stopped, not only would the alcoholic get better, but so would everyone else in the family. Through the ACOA movement, professionals, the public, and adults who grew up in alcoholic homes are becoming more aware of the specific long-term effects of alcoholism. The ACOA's high risk for developing emotional, physical, interpersonal, and behavioral problems (problems which can result in addictive illnesses) is now recognized. Before we explore ACOA family issues more fully, let's take a look at the importance of the family.

The Purpose of a Family

It's through a family that we are taught basic beliefs, values, and a definition of what is normal. It's through the family that each child learns who she is and what to expect in life.

A renowned family therapist, Salvador Minuchin, believes the family is one of the most important groups a child has as she grows up. It is through the family that she develops a sense of identity.

From the experiences she has with her family, a woman will make decisions (both unconscious and conscious) about her identity, her goals in life, and even the type of social groups she can depend on and associate with.

The family and its patterns of interaction influence children and how they learn to function. It is the family that teaches each of us how to think, act, feel, and communicate our thoughts and feelings. A family has a set of rules, and each member has responsibilities that help all members stick to the rules.

In a healthy family, this system would be referred to as an *open family system*. An open family system has rules to live by, but these rules are open for discussion and can be flexible. Each family member has the right to express thoughts and feelings even when other family members don't agree. This does not mean the rules will change, but it does mean the disagreeing family member continues to be respected and accepted, even though she has a different opinion. In an open family system, no one person has all the power. No one person's needs are valued as more important than anyone else's.

A child growing up in an open family system often develops a sense of her identity, has a positive self-image, and feels that her thoughts and feelings are accepted. She learns how to communicate her thoughts and feelings openly and directly but with consideration for others. A person growing up in an open family system knows how to interact with others and how to get her needs met in a healthy fashion.

The Closed Family

Not all family systems are open. Many families operate as a *closed family system*. A closed family system develops when family members, for whatever reason, are inflexible and can't tolerate change and conflict.

The reasons a family feels unable to be open may vary. It can be because a family member has a secret or an illness others are afraid or ashamed of. Perhaps the family has too many rules as it tries to fulfill what it believes are society's expectations.

Whatever the reason, a closed family system is not very good to be a part of; it doesn't allow its members to question the family rules or to voice any thoughts or feelings that contradict those rules. Its members rarely disagree, for fear of being rejected.

A child who grows up in a closed family system doesn't learn to communicate openly and directly. She doesn't learn she can disagree with others and still be respected and accepted. She doesn't learn who she is, what she likes and doesn't like, or how to get her needs met.

Instead, she learns to avoid conflict (peace at any price), to repress her thoughts and feelings so others are not angry or upset, and to be constantly afraid of rejection by the family (low self-esteem and fear of abandonment). These ways of relating are the foundation of codependency, which, as defined in the Introduction, results from being exposed for a period of time to a set of oppressive rules that prevent a person from openly expressing her thoughts, feelings, and problems in a healthy way.

It is easy to see that a closed family system is a codependent family system. The severity of the codependency depends on many things, but the major factor is how long the family continues to operate in a closed, repressive way.

For example, when a family member has a chronic illness, such as cancer, the rest of the family may function as a codependent family system, reacting to the pain and fear of the possible loss of a loved one. Initially, they may avoid discussing their feelings about the illness or deny the severity of the illness. If the family previously functioned as an open family system, they will probably return to being open after the initial pain and fear subside.

In families where one family member is alcoholic and the pain and fear is chronic and progressive over an extended period of time, the codependent way of relating is prolonged—often over a lifetime. Once a person grows up relating to the world in a codependent fashion, she continues to do so unless she receives outside help.

It is difficult for the codependent person to ask for help. No matter what role she played in her family, she learned to follow a specific set of rules. Her self-image and identity are often based on those rules and her role in the family. Her fears are often based on not wanting to risk being unacceptable to others, as was her childhood fear of being rejected or forgotten by her family. She often has a distorted view of reality because of rigid family rules, and lacks assertiveness and has poor communication skills. Because she was rarely or never given the opportunity to express herself openly, she probably doesn't know an effective way to solve problems or manage stress during times when the family rules don't apply to the situation at hand.

Rather than seeking people who challenge her codependent way of living, she finds comfort in relationships with people who have the same codependent lifestyle.

Codependency is often carried from generation to generation. Codependent mothers teach their children by example to be codependent. They also teach their grandchildren to be codependent. The codependent way of relating to others continues until someone gets help to stop the vicious cycle.

The Alcoholic Family

An alcoholic family is often a codependent family. The

disease of alcoholism often creates shame, guilt, and pain for the alcoholic and the entire family. Although alcoholism is a disease, many people still mistakenly view it as a sin or a sign of moral weakness.

The alcoholic's spouse, friends, or significant other all tend to react to the situation in the same way as the alcoholic: everyone experiences *denial.* Denial is a way to avoid pain and conflict. Avoiding pain and conflict for a prolonged period of time can result in rigid family rules. These rules are a futile attempt to keep the family secure so it can continue to appear to be an open family system. The family members want to think they're okay and normal and they want everyone else to think so too.

The alcoholic family is frightened of not being "normal." In reaction to this fear, each family member develops and strictly follows his or her role in the family. The family roles are like life preservers: if you hold on tightly enough, everything will be all right. Each role is an attempt to hide the alcoholism and to keep the family looking normal and in control. We will describe the roles of members of families where alcoholism exists more completely later in this chapter.

As the alcoholism progresses and the alcoholic loses more and more control, the family experiences more chaos. Each family member feels less in control and more afraid that the family secret will be discovered. This makes each member hold tighter to his or her individual life preserver (family role) and thus focuses more attention and energy on the alcoholic.

Roles of the Alcoholic and the Enabler

Alcoholism is a family disease. The disease begins with the alcoholic and his partner, the enabler. Just as the alcoholic battles with himself as the disease progresses and becomes more chronic, the enabler fights the alcoholic's drinking as she begins to experience powerlessness and the loss of the goals she had hoped the relationship would develop and achieve.

Although both husband and wife battle the same enemy—alcoholism—they end up battling each other. The shame, frustration, and powerlessness the alcoholic lives with is projected onto the enabler. Trying to relieve the pressures he is enduring, the alcoholic blames his wife for his feelings and failures, including his drinking. He might criticize her personality, her physical attractiveness (including her sexual desirability), and her competence. This behavior is mixed with apologies, consoling behaviors, and attempts to "win back" her approval and affection.

In response, the enabler takes over more and more of the alcoholic's responsibilities that once gave him a sense of self-worth. She tries to control his drinking while covering up and denying to others that he has a problem. She, too, experiences shame, frustration, and powerlessness and projects this onto the alcoholic. She might criticize his personality, his physical attractiveness (including his sexual prowess), and his competence.

While both partners have many of the same emotions, the alcoholism drives a greater wedge between them. They each become unable to see themselves or the other clearly. The focus of the alcoholic couple's life is the alcoholism. All else is secondary—jobs, friends, and even their children.

The children of alcoholics are born into a chaotic family system that entangles them in the alcoholism. This is an inevitable side effect of alcoholism. The parents don't intend that to happen; it's probably the most distant thing from their minds. Children find ways to try to help their parents meet their needs. They do this by taking on roles assigned by their parents.

The Characteristics—
traits, feelings, and behaviors of Children of Alcoholics

The name of the game or the mode of survival	What you see or Visible traits. Outside behavior.	What you don't see or the inside story. Feelings.	What he/she represents to the family & why they play along.	As an adult without help, this is very possible.	As an adult with help, this is also very possible
THE FAMILY HERO OR SUPER KID	"The little mother." "The little man of the family." Always does what's right, overachiever, over-responsible, needs everyone's approval. Not much fun.	Hurt, inadequate, confusion, guilt, fear, low self-esteem. Progressive disease, so never can do enough.	Provides self-worth to the family, someone to be proud of.	Workaholic, never wrong, marry a dependent person, need to control & manipulate, compulsive, can't say no, can't fail.	Competent, organized, responsible, make good managers. Become successful and healthy.
THE SCAPEGOAT OR PROBLEM KID	Hostility & defiance, withdrawn & sullen, gets negative attention, *troublemaker*.	Hurt & abandoned, anger and rejection, feels totally inadequate and no/low self-worth.	Take the heat. "See what *he's done*." — "Leave me alone."	Alcoholic or addict, unplanned pregnancy, cops and prisons. TROUBLE. Legal trouble.	Recovery, has courage, good under pressure, can see reality, can help others. Can take risks.
THE LOST CHILD	Loner, daydreamer, solitary, (alone rewards, i.e. food), withdrawn, drifts and floats through life, not missed or given up. quiet, shy, ignored.	Unimportant, not allowed to have feelings, loneliness, hurt and abandoned, defeated and given up.	Relief, at least one kid no one worries about.	Indecisive, no little fun, stays the same, alone or promiscuous, dies early, can't say NO.	Independent, talented & creative. Imaginative, assertive & resourceful.
THE MASCOT or FAMILY CLOWN	Supercute, immature and any thing for a laugh or attention; fragile and needful of protection, hyperactive, short attention span, learning disabilities, anxious.	Low self-esteem, terror, lonely, inadequate and unimportant.	Comic relief, fun and humor.	Compulsive clown, lampshade on head, etc. Can't handle stress, marry a "hero," always on verge of hysterics.	Charming host & person, good with company, quick wit, good sense of humor, independent. Helpful.

Excerpted From: CHOICEMAKING, by Sharon Wegscheider-Cruse, (Health Communications, 1985), Nurturing Networks, 2820 West Main Street, Rapid City, South Dakota, 57702, (605) 341-7432.

Roles of Children of Alcoholics

Much has been written (by such people as Claudia Black, Virginia Satir, and Sharon Wegscheider-Cruse) on the roles played by children in alcoholic families. Each role has its characteristics and purposes. Each role is an attempt by children to adapt to the family's alcoholism. As time goes on, the child of an alcoholic parent is trapped in her role and in the expectations the family has for her.

Each of these roles, as defined in the chart on page 13, serves a purpose. In its own way, each role reflects what the alcoholic family is needing and feeling. The alcoholism and codependency has the family living with the myth that it needs to hide the problem and force the feelings to go away. What the family really needs is to face the reality of the drinking and confront the pain, anger, and confusion it creates.

A child takes on one of these roles as a way to adjust to her environment. She makes these adjustments to help Mom and Dad protect and preserve the family's way of operating.

At the time, the child has no way of knowing she is helping to preserve the codependent family system, which ultimately harms everyone. Instead, she is doing whatever she can to survive within the family.

Characteristics of Adult Children of Alcoholics

Children who grow up in alcoholic families are affected by the alcoholism in various ways. A great deal depends on each child's role in the family, along with the severity of the alcoholism, which parent is alcoholic, and the child's age when the alcoholism moves into its later stages. Growing up with an alcoholic mother who doesn't provide basic food and shelter needs when a young child is three or four has a different effect than with a mother whose alcoholism begins later in her life, after the child is a self-sufficient adult.

In spite of these differences, professionals recognize certain personality traits that create problems in the ACOA's life. These include

- perfectionism;
- oversensitivity;
- negativity;
- self-centered;
- having difficulty with change;
- having difficulty with intimacy;
- being overcritical;
- being over- or underresponsible;
- impulsive; and
- having to seek approval.

In *Guide to Recovery,* Herbert Gravitz and Julie Bowden cite nine issues they describe as the most common personal issues adult children of alcoholics struggle with from childhood, through adolescence, and into adulthood. The issues include

- control;
- distrust;
- avoiding feelings;
- overly responsible;
- ignoring one's own needs;
- all-or-nothing thinking;
- dissociation (avoiding one's feelings and needs);
- crisis-oriented; and
- extremely low self-esteem.

Let's look at each of these issues more fully.

Control

ACOAs are frequently referred to as survivors. This term is appropriate when it's more fully understood what skills a child in an alcoholic family must develop to adjust to her environment.

Children learn to be hyperalert if that's the entire

family's style of living. They become hypersensitive to what goes on outside of themselves. They're always concerned about what other people are thinking and doing. They're rarely concerned about what is happening inside of them. They are only concerned with what they're doing in terms of how others think of them or behave toward them.

Being hyperalert requires a child to develop skills of anticipation and manipulation. When growing up in an alcoholic household, a child frequently can't know with certainty what will happen from one day or one moment to the next.

In order to feel some sense of security and self-preservation, family members scan the environment for even the slightest clues to anticipate what may be happening now or what the family moods and interactions may be building up to. Consequently, family members heighten their awareness levels and can anticipate people's behaviors in order to manipulate the environment as well as each other.

Manipulation keeps the family together and united in their efforts to keep the family looking "normal" to the outside world. Each family member's style of manipulation is determined by the role she plays and the types of personal needs she feels must be fulfilled.

The anticipation and manipulation are used by the alcoholic family to feel in control. It keeps each family member focused *externally*. The child who grows up in this family might, as an adult, be overly sensitive, perfectionistic, people-pleasing, and passive in her relationships with others. She did not learn how to be assertive, how to solve problems and manage stress; nor did she learn how to identify and express her personal needs, or how to develop and participate in intimate relationships.

Distrust

The distrust the ACOA feels is not only of others, but of herself as well. As the alcoholism progresses and the family is more controlled by chaos and denial of the disease, the children experience the following:

1. *Lack of confidence.* The children are told what they see and even feel is wrong. This makes them question their perceptions, fostering long-lasting internal confusion and frustration.

2. *Broken promises.* Children in alcoholic families are often promised things by their parents that never come true. Though the sincerity of an alcoholic father's promise to take his son or daughter to a movie after work may be real, his ability to say no to a beer on the way home from work may not be within his power any longer. Mom often cannot be there for the soccer game because she has to pick up Dad so he won't try to drive home drunk. This creates an attitude in the child of "don't count on anyone or anything, you'll just be disappointed."

3. *Inconsistency.* Alcoholic families may be rigid, but they're not consistent. What is okay for the child to do one day may not be okay the next. Continuity and being able to depend on people and things are fundamental to a child's ability to develop trust. Since consistent behavior is frequently absent in an alcoholic household, feelings of distrust become the norm.

Avoiding Feelings

For an alcoholic family to function, it's often important that family members learn to avoid their feelings. Otherwise, their denial system may be broken and the family's worst fear—that there's a problem and other people will find out about it—will happen.

Children are told directly and indirectly not to express themselves. A slapped face when a young daughter voices her anger about her father's drinking or even a gentle "don't feel that way" statement from a parent teaches family members that genuine feelings are wrong, bad, or inappropriate.

Ultimately, the result for the child is not knowing how to identify, tolerate, or express emotions as an adult.

Overly Responsible

By nature, all children are self-centered; thus, they believe they have a greater influence over things than they really do. Children in alcoholic families often grow up feeling responsible for the chaos in the family. Sometimes they are told they are responsible: "If you didn't upset me so much, I wouldn't have to drink to calm down."

Other times, they are given the message more indirectly through the anticipation and manipulation process. For example, a mother who tells her adolescent daughter, "I'm glad we're so close. If it weren't for you I don't know what I'd do." She is telling her daughter that she is responsible for her mother's emotional well-being. If, when the daughter grows up, she moves away and develops a personal identity, Mother will probably fall apart. The mother is really telling the adolescent, "If I fall apart, it will be all your fault because you left me." Consequently, the child grows up feeling overly responsible for the feelings, attitudes, and actions of others. This begins as the child grows up in the family and gets transferred to all her other relationships.

Ignoring One's Own Needs

Children in an alcoholic family learn to disregard their own needs early in life. It doesn't take very long for the child to discover that what she needs is always secondary to the alcoholic's needs. Ignoring her own needs becomes a well-developed survival skill for the child.

For example, if Mom needs to sleep off a hangover and the child needs new clothes, Mom gets to sleep off the hangover first. As time goes on, the child may begin to view her needs as selfish or deny they exist. It's easier for a child to feel guilty over being selfish or pretend to be tough or pretend her needs don't really matter than it is for the child to admit she may be unloved by her parents.

As this child grows into adulthood, she is inclined to continue ignoring her own needs without realizing she continues to carry her feelings of inadequacy and a pervasive sense of unfulfillment.

All-or-Nothing Thinking

The rigidity of the alcoholic family creates a lifestyle of extremes. Children witness and are a part of emotional extremes (explosive anger or cold silences) and physical extremes (hitting, extreme affection, or no touching at all). The inability to talk about what is going on and how people feel leads the adult child to see things in black and white, as being either right or wrong. This gives her a sense of personal empowerment. This attitude usually creates a sense of being out of control because the child doesn't have the skills needed to handle more complex problems for which clear-cut answers are less apparent.

For example, a child growing up with an alcoholic parent may label anger as bad and believe the only way anger can be expressed is in an explosive way—screaming, name-calling, throwing things, or hitting. Such a child may think, *I'll never get angry and be like that!* This is her way of being in control and being good. She cuts off all emotions related to anger. She labels other people who express anger as *bad*. This gives her an excuse to avoid angry or hostile people and deny her own angry feelings. She feels a false sense of power as she tries to control herself and her environment. The person who denies anger has a difficult time being assertive and getting her needs met.

Dissociation

Dissociation is a way to avoid feelings and ignore one's personal needs. As a survival skill for a child living in an alcoholic home, dissociation blocks out pain. For the adult child of an alcoholic, dissociation continues to block pain, but it keeps her unable to understand why she gets involved in unhealthy relationships or has bouts of depression, anxiety, or explosive anger.

For example, while a child is being screamed at and demeaned by the alcoholic parent, she escapes by daydreaming. She then withdraws to her room to play alone. She has removed herself from the chaos and from her feelings because the hurt and fear of her parent's criticism is too much to handle. In her mind, the screaming didn't occur.

Crisis-oriented

For better or worse, what we become familiar with in our families is what we are most comfortable with. Alcoholic families operate on a crisis-to-crisis basis. Often, these crises are a way for the nonalcoholic family members to temporarily bond together and communicate more than they typically would.

For example, Mom and Dad are having a big fight, and Dad storms out of the house saying he's never coming back. Everyone in the house responds to his behavior in a different way depending on their role in the family.

In taking this example a step further, let's say Dad was involved in a serious automobile accident after leaving home. The family suddenly rises to the occasion and bonds together to visit him in the hospital and takes care of things at home in his absence.

This familiarity with crises and the sense of belonging that often goes with it are carried into the adult child's life. This may be prevalent in her choice of relationships (many ACOAs marry alcoholics), her money management skills, and even her choice of professions (nurses and doctors working in intensive care units and emergency rooms; businesses with high-risk investments; social workers for a crisis hotline; children's protective services; or working in psychiatric emergency rooms).

Extremely Low Self-esteem

The ACOAs we see in treatment may appear to be able to cope with day-to-day life, but underneath is their inability to express feelings and personal needs. They often suffer from a pervasive sense of shame, guilt, self-denial, over-responsibility, and distrust. This keeps them seeing themselves as out of control, inadequate, unworthy, and unable to handle life.

Summary

In this chapter, we have discussed how families operate, the importance of the family system, and the emotional growth and development of its children.

An open family system provides nurturing and values, self-acceptance, self-responsibility, and self-confidence in each family member. A closed family system is focused on maintaining an unhealthy status quo at the expense of its individual members.

As a closed family system, the alcoholic family suffers from both alcoholism and codependency. All family members suffer and struggle with the emotional, interpersonal, behavioral, and physical symptoms and side effects of these addictions.

Though ACOAs are survivors, they are disabled veterans in many ways. They carry with them the wounds and scars of their battle with the family's alcoholism and codependency long after leaving the battlefield. Without help to recover, they often continue to fight the battle alone, carrying it into each life situation and relationship.

The ACOA who does not enter a recovery program will most likely continue to be controlled by the personality characteristics and lifestyle patterns we have described in this chapter.

How ACOAs attempt to cope varies from individual to individual. Our experience has taught us that many try to cope through using behaviors that may become addictive. Compulsive eating, in the form of overeating or bingeing and purging is one of the coping skills that can numb the pain.

CHAPTER
-2-

Compulsive Eating: The Culture, the Family, the Individual

Food can be a source of sustenance and pleasure. It does more than satiate hunger; it is the main event at celebrations like birthdays, baptisms, even funerals. For many people, growing food in the backyard garden and cooking are enjoyable hobbies.

Sometimes people use food to cope. When a person feels sad or depressed, a scoop of ice cream or some potato chips can be soothing. When anxiety strikes, cookies may serve as a way to reduce the tension. Once the uncomfortable feeling passes, the individual resumes normal eating patterns.

For some people, however, normal eating does not resume. The good feelings from eating reinforce its use time and time again. A love-trust relationship is established; food initially fills a need that is not being met. This behavior usually results in weight gain or a fear of weight gain. Consequently, the individual may turn to dieting or other means to regain control and to lose weight.

A change in the body occurs. When a person diets, the body adjusts to a lower calorie intake; the metabolic rate slows down, and it becomes easier to add more pounds. So the more times a person diets, the harder it becomes to lose weight. This can lead to more bingeing and purging, an activity marked by a tremendous intake of food followed by ridding the body of calories or weight, usually through induced vomiting, use of laxatives, or even excessive exercise. What originally felt good—eating—has now taken on a life of its own. A person who has this type of a relationship with food is a compulsive eater. For the compulsive eater, food is an addiction and, as with any addiction, it becomes the major focus in the person's life.

For example, compulsive eaters often avoid social engagements that involve eating if they are on a diet. Or they may binge before or after a social event, coming late or leaving early. In daily conversations with people, they are often mentally absent because they are thinking about what they have eaten or what they will be eating.

There are many similarities between compulsive eating and alcoholism. Compulsive eating can be as addictive as alcohol; it is a chronic, progressive disease and, like alcohol, not only harms the victim but everyone around her. The Jellinek Chart, which illustrates the progressive nature of alcoholism, is adapted here to show a similar progression in the disease of compulsive eating.

Compulsive eaters consume huge quantities of food rapidly (binge eating) and secretly. For example, a binge might consist of two dozen cookies, a pint or two of ice cream, and several candy bars. This binge feels pleasurable while the person is gorging. Once the person stops eating, however, she is consumed with overwhelming feelings of guilt, remorse, and self-hate. She has a strong urge to regain control and does so by purging her body (fasting, rigid dieting, laxative abuse, or vomiting).

Compulsive eaters are driven by a desire to be thin. This obsession makes compulsive eaters easy prey for fad diets or "miracle" weight loss schemes. Buying books, consuming pills, and going to weight loss programs which require special foods are ways that compulsive eaters search for a miraculous cure.

CHART ONE

A Chart of Eating Addiction and Recovery

Early

- Occasional relief eating (or fasting)
- Constant relief eating (or fasting) commences
- Onset of memory "fuzziness"
- Increasing dependence on food or dieting
- Feelings of guilt
- Difficulty determining feelings of fullness
- Decrease of ability to stop compulsive eating behaviors
- Grandiose passive/aggressive behaviors
- Efforts to control fall repeatedly
- Try geographical escapes
- Avoid family and friends
- Unreasonable resentments
- Loss of ordinary willpower
- Changes in food tolerance
- Onset of lengthy "intoxications"
- Impaired thinking
- Indefinable fears
- Obsession with eating, weight, dieting
- All alibis exhausted

Middle

- Surreptitious eating
- Urgency for food or compulsive exercise
- Unable to discuss problem
- Eating behavior bolstered with excuses
- Persistent remorse
- Loss of other interests
- Work and money troubles
- Neglect of proper nutrition
- Physical deterioration
- Moral deterioration
- Unable to initiate action
- Vague spiritual desires
- Complete defeat admitted

Late

- Physical examination by physician
- Learn disease concept
- Assisted in exploring life conflicts
- Rationalizations recognized
- Diminishing fears of the unknown
- Physical nourishment improves
- Natural rest and sleep returns
- Developing sense of self-acceptance
- Break patterns of physical and emotional Isolation
- Increasing emotional stability
- Sense of contentment develops
- Continuation of involvement in aftercare and support groups

- Honest desire for help
- Begin treatment program
- Told addiction can be arrested
- Spiritual needs examined
- Develop abstinence concept
- Onset of new hope
- Returning self-esteem
- Desire to escape lessens
- Adjusting to family needs
- New interests develop
- Increasing willingness to take risks
- Increasing economic stability

Obsessive eating continues in vicious circles

Adapted from the Jellinek Chart

Compulsive eaters are forever dieting, forever counting calories, and forever battling with their feelings about food.

They feel deprived much of the time. They are resentful and angry because they aren't like other people when it comes to food. They feel there is something radically wrong with them and try to hide their problems with food from others. They feel a deep sense of shame and embarrassment.

Compulsive eaters equate thinness with success and being in control. Consequently, they think in terms of "if only's." "If only I were thinner, then I would get that promotion." "If only I were thinner, then I would be married." Being thin is the dream of dreams; it means everything will be wonderful.

Although we use the term *compulsive eaters* to identify individuals who have the disease, we believe there are really two types of compulsive eaters—those who are average weight (often referred to as bulimic) and those who are overweight (often referred to as obese). Despite some differences, there is one basic similarity: compulsive eaters are out of control when it comes to food. (See Chart 2 on the following pages.)

Purging for the average weight compulsive eater might consist of vomiting, abusing laxatives or diuretics, frantic exercising, fasting, or rigid dieting. Because compulsive eaters offset the huge caloric intake with some form of purging, their weight only fluctuates by ten to fifteen pounds.

Overweight compulsive eaters' purging is not consistent, so their binges result in weight gain. The form of purging they rely on most is dieting. Those who are average weight are often diet junkies on a continual diet roller coaster.

Compulsive Overeating

BEHAVIORAL

- 20 percent or more overweight
- bingeing
- diet junkie
- weight gain/loss roller coaster
- hides and sneaks food
- may have genetic predisposition to obesity

PSYCHOLOGICAL

- lack of awareness of feelings
- unassertive
- strong need to please others
- need to control
- strong need for others' approval
- low self-esteem
- powerlessness
- depression
- superficial relationships
- difficulty expressing anger or disagreement
- strong need to take care of others— martyr role
- shame-based existence

PHYSICAL

- gallstones
- degenerative joint disease
- circulatory problems
- hormonal imbalance
- sleep apnea (momentary suspension of respiration while sleeping)
- other respiratory problems
- diabetes
- hypertension
- cardiovascular disease
- breast cancer
- decreased life expectancy

Bulimia

BEHAVIORAL

- cyclical pattern of bingeing and purging
- vomiting
- laxative abuse
- fasting
- rigid dieting
- secret eating
- prone to substance abuse, such as diuretic abuse (drugs that increase the discharge of urine)
- shoplifting
- suicidal behavior
- likely to have been sexually abused or raped

PSYCHOLOGICAL

- represses feelings, especially anger
- hypersensitive to criticism
- strong feelings of powerlessness and depression
- impulsive
- tends to isolate self, has difficulty with intimate relationships
- secretive
- shame-based existence
- low self-esteem
- obsession with food, weight, physical appearance, control
- strong need for others' approval

PHYSICAL

- irregular menstruation or amenorrhea
- dehydration: dry skin, brittle nails and hair
- fainting
- constant thirst
- dizziness
- electrolyte imbalance
- muscle weakness
- muscle cramping
- dental problems: dental care, enamel erosion
- parotid (salivary glands located below and in front of ear) enlargement
- intolerance to colds
- fatigue
- digestive difficulties
- abdominal pain
- constipation

CHART TWO
(Part Three)

Anorexia Nervosa

BEHAVIORAL	PSYCHOLOGICAL	PHYSICAL
• refuses to maintain recommended minimal weight	• no real sense of a self	• irregular menstruation or amenorrhea (absence or suppression of mentrual discharge)
• eating rituals	• obsession with food, weight control	• low blood pressure
• frenetic exercise	• isolation	• slow heartbeat
• denies food-related problems	• secretiveness	• extremeties— vulnerable to cold
• high mortality rate	• feels fat; distorted body image	• vulnerable to infection
• irritability	• fear of food	• self-inflicted weight loss
• mood swings	• suppression of hunger	• constipation
• indecisiveness	• depression	• bloating, abdominal pain
• obsessive thinking		• lethargy, bursts of energy
		• anemia (listless and weak)

Compulsive eaters have a distorted body image. An average-weight compulsive eater often feels fat, although in reality she is not. The overweight compulsive eater suffers from the added pressure of being fat. The compulsive eaters who are average weight fit the cultural norm of being thin. Being ten or fifteen pounds overweight is acceptable, but being 80 or 90 pounds overweight is definitely not.

The overweight compulsive eater suffers additional blows to her self-esteem. The overeating is obvious to the naked eye. People who are fat are criticized, rejected, seen as lazy or having no self-discipline. Knowing she doesn't meet cultural expectations contributes to her feelings of inadequacy and worthlessness.

Compulsive eaters, regardless of weight, generally share the following common traits:

- they feel worthless and powerless;
- they have a strong need to control their world;
- they have difficulty expressing feelings, especially anger;
- they have confused feelings about their sexuality;
- they have difficulty in intimate relationships;
- they have a distorted body image; and
- they are perfectionistic.

Eating Disorders Are on the Rise

There seem to be more and more people seeking help for compulsive eating. Incidents of bingeing and purging have increased dramatically in the last five to ten years.

Surveys among college women reveal that 75 percent or more describe themselves as binge eaters, and 4 to 8 percent admit that they have vomited on at least one occasion to deal with overeating.

Over 50 million Americans exceed by ten percent or more their ideal body weight and therefore can be considered obese; 15 million Americans are so obese that their health is seriously at risk.

Why Now?

Bingeing has been a problem for some overweight people for many years. It has always been assumed that overweight people have merely been unable to control themselves. It has been especially difficult in the last ten years for overweight people to deal with cultural expectations, as fitness has become the norm.

It's not coincidental that eating disorders have been on the rise in the last decade and continue to be a major health problem. There are cultural shifts in male and female roles that impact each of us and how we relate to each other in our multiple roles as spouse, mother, father, daughter, son, employee.

In examining the rise of eating disorders, it's important to look at the individual and all the factors that influence growth and development. Chart Three on page 32 illustrates the scope of the influencing factors.

EATING DISORDERS AND THE CULTURE

Cultural Expectations Regarding Thinness

Femininity is often equated with being fragile, thin, small, and delicate. These images conflict with viewing women as powerful, strong, and credible. Usually big women are seen as less than feminine.

For decades, women have tried to be small and petite. They have sacrificed their well-being to be more acceptable. In the 1900s, for example, women suffered immense pain when wearing whalebone corsets, which sometimes caused broken ribs. These undergarments allowed women to have the feminine hourglass figure popular during that cultural period. Some of them even had surgery to remove lower ribs so they could be even more acceptable and admired.

American women were not the only ones to endure physical pain for the cultural vision of beauty. The Chinese bound little girls' feet to stunt growth and give the appearance of delicacy.

The message is clear: "You are not acceptable as you are. You should be and look like . . ." In the fifties, it was Marilyn Monroe; in the sixties and seventies, it was Jackie Kennedy and Twiggy; and in the eighties, it's Jane Fonda.

CHART THREE

Personality Development

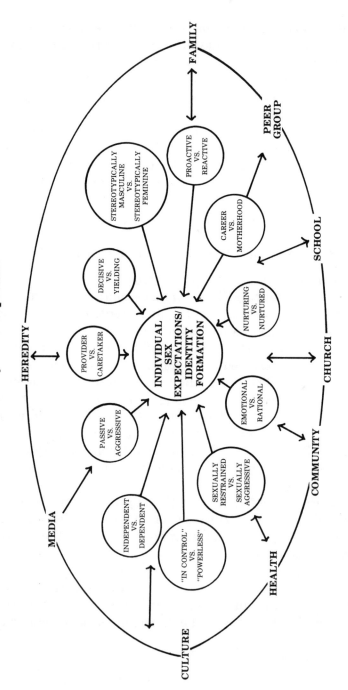

The individual's sex role expectations and identity are developed through her attempts to resolve the conflicts posed by the characteristics as pictured above. The definition of these characteristics and how "good" or "bad" they are perceived to be are influenced by the elements of the outer circle.

Women have been raised to believe their power rests in their beauty and kindness. Society has fostered the idea that the feminine ideal is passive, beautiful, thin, kind, self-sacrificing, and loving. This cultural belief has a significant impact on how women learn to function in the workplace and in relationships. *It teaches them to be passive in getting their needs met.*

It is impossible to always be giving, kind, and loving and to know exactly when and how much. One area that is controllable in a more tangible way is weight. She can see the numbers on the scale, she can count the calories, she can feel a size ten on her size fourteen body, but she can't measure how much kindness or love to give, or how extensively she should sacrifice herself.

Thinness is an easier way to measure success. The culture and media keep brainwashing us with images of thin, beautiful women who seem to have it all. Women get trapped into believing that their physical appearance and their beauty and kindness will ensure that their needs will be met and life will be wonderful.

Cultural Definitions of Femininity

Developing femininity successfully today requires that women meet three basic demands:

- she must defer to others;
- she must anticipate the needs of others; and
- she must seek self-definition through her relationships.

Women are encouraged to deny themselves; consequently, they are unable to develop a sense of what their needs are. They are preoccupied with taking care of everyone else and are unfamiliar with their own needs. Because of this, women depend on those they give to for approval and validation. They are discouraged from expressing their dependency needs and from taking action. They are encouraged to wait for things to happen to them. If they are good enough, thin enough, and kind enough, they will be taken care of. Women have been raised to be there for others. If the "others" don't respond and meet their needs, they feel they have failed.

Before the women's movement and the hard realities of our economy, a woman had to worry about keeping her parents, her children, and her husband happy and content with her. That has changed as she has moved into the marketplace. She is being encouraged to think in terms of career and lifetime work in addition to other demanding responsibilities at home.

Now she has to make sure she keeps her boss and her co-workers happy and content with her as well. She may run from home to work to home again, taking care of everybody, hoping someone will take care of her. The anger and resentment build as she becomes exhausted, but she feels like a failure if she complains or can't handle it all.

Young women today are faced with more choices than their mothers and strive to have the best of both worlds—family and career. This has placed great stress on them because now they feel they must succeed in both places. Feeling the pressures of being a good wife and mother and a responsible employee contribute to the "superwoman syndrome."

Women who have accepted and internalized the social and cultural beliefs about thinness and attractiveness are more likely to become compulsive eaters. Women who have not come to terms with what being feminine means to them are also more likely to become compulsive eaters. *Compulsive eating results from struggling to live up to an ideal of femininity.*

EATING DISORDERS AND THE FAMILY

The culture's expectations of both men and women place a great deal of stress on people's ability to have intimate relationships. Our culture fosters an unequal distribution of power between the male and female and may make it more likely for a daughter to develop an eating disorder.

A couple's inability to relate to each other on an equal basis often results in the mother pulling the children into a closer relationship with her. This offsets the emptiness she feels within her marriage. The father, consequently, feels left out and will distance himself through work, alcohol, or outside activities as he tries to have his needs met and feel a sense of belonging.

As a result of this triangle between father, mother, and children, the family develops unhealthy styles of relating.

The authors of the book, *Bulimia: A Systems Approach to Treatment,* say that eating disorder families can fall into one of three types of families.

The Perfect Family places importance on appearances, the family's reputation, the family's identity, and achievement. They are overly concerned with how they are seen by the community.

The Overprotective Family emphasizes a need to be close. They tend to take too much responsibility for the family members, particularly a family member with a problem.

The Chaotic Family has neither parent available to the children. Rules are inconsistent or nonexistent. The children learn not to talk, trust, or feel.

These families described above are commonly alcoholic families. Typically, these families can be characterized as:

1. *Having a difficult time letting the children grow up and leave home.* This dysfunctional family experiences tremendous stress when the children either move into adolescence (when anorexia or compulsive eating usually surface), or when the adolescent moves into young adulthood (when bulimia or compulsive eating usually surface). Given the rigid rules and the empty relationship between mother and father, it is difficult for the child to make the

necessary changes to gain more independence. The mother sees this as a move away from her.

2. *Having a difficult time establishing boundaries.* Boundaries mean that families provide physical space and privacy for its members. Eating disorder families have difficulty finding a balance between the individual "I's" and the collective family "we's." "We are one" is the family motto. This "we" makes it difficult for members to identify their individual needs, strengths, and abilities.

3. *Having a difficult time establishing flexible rules.* Rules create order and are important because they can either help a person establish a sense of competence and self-sufficiency or render her powerless. Rules in the eating disorder family are confusing, conflicting, or extremely rigid. Such rules might include:

- don't talk about our problems to the outside world;
- don't do anything that would make the family ashamed; and
- always think of your parents' feelings first.

4. *Having a difficult time determining what feelings are acceptable.* In these families, the child quickly learns which feelings get a positive or negative reaction from her parents. In the eating disorder family, it's usually not okay for people to express feelings. They use lots of "shoulds" and "should nots."

- "You shouldn't feel that way."
- "You should be happy with what you have."
- "You shouldn't just think of yourself all the time."

This gives the youngster the feeling that what she is feeling is bad, wrong, or unacceptable. She then begins to believe that *she* is bad, wrong, or unacceptable.

5. *Placing value on weight and appearance.* The eating

disorder family typically gives the message, either verbally or nonverbally, that weight and appearance are important. They have accepted the culture's expectation about women and femininity. They believe their daughters need to look good and be thin in order to succeed and make them look like successful parents.

THE FUNCTION OF COMPULSIVE EATING

Given this family system, a compulsive eating behavior serves a number of functions.

1. *It can be a safe way to rebel against being perfect.* She can be a compliant, people-pleasing, wonderful daughter while using her compulsive eating or purging as a way to be bad or imperfect. She feels great satisfaction in secretly hurting her perfect image without risking rejection from her family, teachers, and friends.

2. *It's an effective coping mechanism to deal with painful feelings.* The family discourages recognition and expression of feelings, particularly negative feelings, such as anger, guilt, or frustration. Compulsive eating is a way to stuff the feelings, to numb them, to shut them off. Focusing on food shifts attention away from feelings.

3. *It's a way to achieve a sense of identity apart from the family.* The compulsive eating or purging takes on a life of its own. She integrates her relationship with food or purging into the core of her being. It is hers and hers alone.

4. *It's a safe way to express forbidden anger.* Many compulsive eaters binge in response to feeling very angry. The family rule about never feeling anger (which would lead to conflict) and the cultural rule *Nice girls don't get angry* lead the individual to turn the angry feelings onto the self. Bingeing or purging is a physical release from pent up anger while allowing the individual to still be nice and avoid conflict.

5. *It's a way to bring Mom and Dad together.* The com-

pulsive eater discovers that one time her parents communicate with each other is when they are concerned about her weight or her eating patterns. Her compulsive eating becomes a way to reconnect her parents, and, it's hoped, stabilize their relationship. If her parents bond as a couple, she will feel less responsible for taking care of her mother's emotional needs , thereby allowing her the freedom to grow up and leave home.

6. *It's a way to remain childlike.* Compulsive eating behaviors reinforce the youngster's irresponsibility. She is sick and needs her parents to continue to take care of her. The eating disorder keeps her from facing the frightening prospect of leaving home and growing up.

7. *It's a way to feel nurtured.* Food becomes a friend and companion who is always there, no matter what. When lonely, compulsive eating is a way to fill the emptiness. When happy, it's a way to celebrate. Unlike her family, no matter what happens, food doesn't reject or abandon; it can be counted on.

8. *It's a way to experience some predictability.* Given the chaotic family system, both compulsive eating and purging is something the individual has control over initially. No one, but no one, can interfere. It is her domain—the one thing in her life she, and she alone, can control.

9. *It's a way to abuse oneself.* This is particularly true of bulimics. The behavior reinforces her belief that she is unacceptable and inadequate. The violence of purging re-creates feelings of powerlessness she feels so intensely. The compulsive eating and purging is a way to fully experience her self-hate.

EATING DISORDERS AND THE INDIVIDUAL

We have been reviewing compulsive eating in our culture and in families. We will now look at the individual and see how food affects a person as she grows up.

Infancy

Food is the basic means of communication from the first day of life. The feeding relationship between parent and baby not only meets the baby's physical needs; feeding also affects our relationship with food and our understanding of intimacy and closeness. Feeding an infant is an intimate experience. It's a physical exchange between two people. Even though not all mothers breast-feed, there is an emotional intensity during feeding. The mother is responsible for the mood at feeding time; the feelings she brings to the feeding are very important.

The mother's attitude is communicated to the baby. This introduction to food and eating affects the child's later relationship with food.

Mother's self-esteem, her sense of femininity, her relationship with the child's father, her age and maturity level, her sense of economic security, and her relationship with her birth family—especially with her mother—all influence the mother's feeding relationship with the newborn baby.

Childhood

As the infant develops, the feeding relationship changes. The youngster is better able to feed herself and make her own food choices. She establishes food likes and dislikes. Mother and child may disagree about some choices because Mom feels a need to control what the child eats and make sure the child eats nutritionally.

Part of Mom's need to control depends on how effective she feels as a mother. Food preparation has traditionally been a major responsibility for women. It may be through her cooking that she feels a sense of worth as a mother. It's a tangible way to show how much she loves and cares for her child.

As the child becomes older, she has her own ideas about what she will and will not eat. This conflict with food can be managed, or it can develop into a long-term power struggle between mother and child.

The more dysfunctional the parents, the more likely Mother is to overinvest in her children. She is likely to derive a sense of self-worth solely from her role as mother. As her relationship with her husband and herself feels more out of control, she feels more of a need to control her child and be a mother. Food preparation, the child's weight, and the child's food choices can become a battleground. Her self-esteem as a mother is at stake.

Adolescence

The number of adolescents who have eating disorders is dramatically high. They may use food and weight to cope with the physical and emotional stress of this developmental period. Let's examine these stressors more fully.

Physically, moving into adolescence creates a particular problem for girls. Before puberty, girls have 10 to 15 percent more body fat than boys, but after puberty girls have almost twice as much body fat as boys. Girls gain weight at puberty primarily as fat tissue, while boys develop muscle and lean tissue. Physical maturation for boys brings them closer to their idea of being a man. For girls, however, it may mean developing away from their feminine ideal. Adolescent girls are often dissatisfied with their weight and appearance. Being thin, to them, means being popular and acceptable.

Emotionally, adolescents need to develop a sense of independence and a sense of identity apart from their families. This is especially difficult for girls, who, due to cultural expectations, are taught to defer to others, to need others, and to take care of others.

Attempts by them to lose or gain weight may be a refuge from the physical changes they are going through. These changes signal a move into adulthood and into situations that require independence. Losing and gaining weight may be an attempt to defy these bodily changes and adulthood.

Extreme dieting preserves a childlike look, which may reflect a girl's desire to remain a child. It puts the brakes on the transition into adulthood. Severe undereating and bingeing and purging can stop menstruation.

The adolescent who overeats and is overweight, on the other hand, finds safety in her fat—it blurs the curves of her female body. Being overweight keeps her baby-fat image intact.

Both the compulsive eater and the purger don't have to worry about dating, how to act, or what to say in front of peers. Their main focus is on how they look.

Feeling the bulge of a tummy (bloating is common for compulsive eaters who vomit or use laxatives) can be an excuse for not going to a social activity. "I'm just too fat." If she is in fact overweight, she won't go to a social activity because "everyone will stare or laugh at me." Either way, she stays home.

When she stays at home feeling angry or depressed because deep down she knows she is missing out, she will use food to numb the pain. Her isolation fosters two things: First, she doesn't develop a sense of competence and worth. Second, she continues to feel lonely and inadequate because she is not learning the social skills she needs to develop relationships.

Her weight determines whether or not she will become involved in the world around her. Whether she is too fat or only feels too fat, she remains outside of the peer group, never really allowing herself to become too involved.

At home, her weight becomes the symbol of her independence. Given the family dynamics, the adolescent often uses her weight as a sign of her uniqueness and control. She develops her identity around her eating disorder.

COMMON TRAITS

Given the dysfunctional family and our culture and the stresses of growing up amidst these two, the disease of compulsive eating may begin to have a life of its own and becomes a central focus in the girl's identity. Many compulsive eaters have several characteristics in common. Let's look at some of them.

Compulsive eaters generally feel worthless and powerless. Cultural views of women are less than flattering. They are seen as weak, emotional, passive, and indecisive. These cultural beliefs take a toll on the eating disorder family.

In addition to the cultural messages of female weakness, the family tends to be troubled; this encourages the compulsive eater to believe she's incapable of taking care of herself. The compulsive eater's mother, a potent role model, also shows that she, too, needs to be cared for.

Compulsive eaters look to others and depend on others for approval and validation because they don't know how to meet their own needs. They don't even know what their needs are.

Bingeing fuels the sense of powerlessness. On the one hand, bingeing means *I can't control eating. I am a weak person.* On the other hand, the compulsive eater feels powerful and in control when the purging and dieting cycle begins. The conflict continues to weaken her self-esteem.

Compulsive eaters are often overly responsible in relationships. When self-esteem is so low, compulsive eaters don't feel lovable. They work hard at making themselves indispensable. They are often overresponsible in their relationships, doing everything for everybody.

Anger and resentment builds as demands from others increase and the compulsive eater isn't getting what she needs in return. She might believe that *as long as I take care of you, you will meet my unspoken expectations and needs.* When this doesn't happen (and it rarely does) her anger results in a binge. She feels she has failed.

Overly responsible people might act like martyrs. "Look at all I do for you, all I have given up." These words are spoken or implied. This, of course, makes the other person feel guilty and trapped. When the martyr's requests are not met, the compulsive eater resorts to bingeing.

Many compulsive eaters have difficulty expressing feelings. They may have little or no awareness of their feelings, perhaps believing they shouldn't feel anything, especially negative feelings like anger or despair. They learn this in their families.

Some compulsive eaters view feelings as a sign of weakness or imperfection. When strong feelings do emerge, compulsive eaters often see them as a reflection of their weakness, as being out of control. This panics them into a binge. The bingeing helps them avoid their feelings. Then, trying to regain control, they diet.

Avoiding normal feelings keep her in the pendulum of mood swings. When she is in control and on a diet, she feels really good about herself. When she is in a binge cycle she feels depressed and helpless.

Compulsive eaters often have confused feelings about their sexuality. Compulsive eaters are often fearful of sex and of their sexual feelings. For the overweight compulsive eater, her weight shields her from these feelings and protects her from physical intimacy. An average weight compulsive eater may be sexually active, but her only desire may be to please her partner, hoping her partner will take care of her sexual needs. This often doesn't happen, leaving the compulsive eater feeling inadequate and worthless.

Orgasm involves letting oneself go. This is difficult for some compulsive eaters because it means trusting another person. Many compulsive eaters have been so hurt in relationships, beginning with their family of origin, that they fear rejection.

Compulsive eaters also have conflicting feelings about their sex roles. Given the changing sex roles in our culture and the unequal distribution of power in their parents' relationship, many compulsive eaters don't know what's expected of them as women. They are supposed to be feminine and have a family, yet move boldly into the larger world and have a career. This can create confusion.

Compulsive eaters generally have difficulty in intimate relationships. Even though many compulsive eaters are well liked, they rarely feel close to anyone. In their family of origin, acceptance might have been based on behaving a certain way. Thus these compulsive eaters were never able to experience acceptance based on their own personal worth. Consequently, opening up to another person feels risky and dangerous. They fear rejection. Rather than risking being hurt, they don't let people get too close.

Because of their family dynamics, compulsive eaters often have trouble with boundaries in relationships. They tend to take on the other person's feelings without being aware of their own feelings. They might do just about anything for a person they care about, often at the expense of their own needs. This is referred to as *deselfing,* that is, always putting the needs of the other before one's own, and being more concerned about keeping harmony in the relationship at the expense of one's differences.

To be intimate, a person needs a sense of a self; otherwise she fears being swallowed up by the other person. This is another conflict for many compulsive eaters. On the one hand, they might depend heavily on their partner, but at the same time they're afraid of becoming too close or lost in the relationship. This conflict mirrors their inner conflict with dependency and independence.

The companionship with food can replace companionship with people. As compulsive eaters have more and more pain in their relationships, they tend to withdraw and eat.

Most compulsive eaters are future oriented. Compulsive

eaters are almost always thinking about the future: "When I lose weight . . . " "When I get accepted into graduate school. . . " "When I am married . . . " Focusing on future events keeps them from experiencing pain in the present. All these future events are supposed to bring them happiness. When the event occurs, however, they are usually disappointed because the dream is often more exciting than reality.

Compulsive eaters have difficulty expressing anger. Because they need approval and don't want to upset their relationships and risk being alone, compulsive eaters rarely express their anger. Depression becomes "safe" as they turn their anger inward.

Because they try to please others, they agree to do things they really don't want to do. They have difficulty saying no or "I don't want to." They go along with what others want and lose touch with their own needs and desires.

Once she begins to feel her anger, the compulsive eater binges. Not believing it is okay to be angry and to disagree with another person keeps her feeling powerless, worthless, and dependent. It keeps her from discovering her true self.

Compulsive eaters generally have a distorted body image. For women in our culture, having a fit body is equated with being successful, lovable, and in control of life. Compulsive eaters place great emphasis on thinness and see themselves as successful and acceptable as long as they maintain an "ideal" body weight. *If only I were thinner I would be more lovable . . . or powerful . . . or happier.*

Compulsive eaters never feel thin enough. Average weight compulsive eaters feel fat, while those who are overweight minimize their weight. Both distortions keep these people bingeing and full of self-hate. They have set themselves up to always feel as though they are failures.

Compulsive eaters are often perfectionists. Most compulsive eaters believe there is a right way to be that ensures happiness, love from others, and a good life. They continually try to be perfect so they can be happy. This drive for perfection often results in depression and feelings of inadequacy. If they behave less than perfectly they experience deep feelings of failure. For example, if a compulsive eater lets her anger slip out, she feels as though she has failed since she believes she should always be in control, never get upset, be loving, kind, and giving all the time.

This same sense of perfection occurs with food. If she eats one forbidden food and goes off her diet, she binges. She feels she has failed and not measured up to her ideal.

Perfectionism also keeps her from trying new activities and meeting new people. Since she is afraid of failure, she never tries anything she can't do perfectly. Again, she has no sense of working toward a goal. She thinks she should succeed at whatever she tries.

Chart Four summarizes the psychological factors that relate to compulsive eating.

Psychological Factors

SELF-ESTEEM

fragile
no real sense of self
no awareness of personal resources
confusion about sex role expectations
distorted body image (which affects self-esteem)
unrealistic expectations of self
self-critical

FEELINGS

powerlessness
depression
anger
inadequacy and worthlessness
fear
hypersensitivity to criticism
lack of awareness of here-
and-now feelings

RELATIONSHIPS

highly dependent
needs constant approval
superficial
keeps secrets
lack of trust
no sense of boundaries
manipulative/controlling
unrealistic expectations
judgmental/critical of others

CHAPTER
- 3 -

Adult Children of Alcoholics and Compulsive Eating

Our experience has shown a connection between developing an eating disorder and growing up in an alcoholic family.

As discussed in Chapter One, anyone who lives in a repressed family system—a family that doesn't let its members go through the emotional and behavioral changes necessary to grow up—is likely to become codependent. Codependents and compulsive eaters have several characteristics in common. They include

- perfectionism;
- the need to be in control;
- people pleasing;
- low self-esteem;
- false pride;
- difficulty with intimacy; and
- difficulty expressing and experiencing emotions.

PREDISPOSING FACTORS

Not all ACOAs develop an eating disorder, but a large percentage of them do. What makes the difference? In addition to the emotional repression in the family, other factors in the family affect whether or not a child develops an eating disorder. These include

- the child's emotional development and the severity of the alcoholism;
- how rigidly the parents follow traditional sex-role behaviors and attitudes;
- the family's value on food and weight; and
- the child's level of emotional involvement in the family system.

Let's examine each factor more fully.

The Child's Emotional Development/ Severity of the Alcoholism

Emotional and cognitive development for the human being occurs in stages. Each stage is characterized by a specific conflict that must be mastered so adequate development can take place. Each successive stage acts as a building block for the next stage. For example, in cognitive development, a child must master addition before multiplication. Multiplication skills will prepare for mastery of division.

Emotional development works in a similar fashion. Mastery of each stage is a way to achieve emotional maturity. In the alcoholic family, it is extremely difficult for children to master any stage of emotional development because not only are they faced with the task itself but they must also withstand the stresses of living in an alcoholic family environment. Robert J. Ackerman, in his book *Children of Alcoholics,* discusses how alcoholism can negatively influence the stages of emotional development for ACOAs.

Erik Erikson developed a theory for the stages of emotional growth. Using Erikson's stages of emotional development, we will discuss how the alcoholic system can promote the development of an eating disorder in a child.

Stage One (1 Year Old)—Trust Versus Mistrust

Erikson believed that a person's ability to trust was a cornerstone in the development of a healthy personality. For a child, basic elements of trust are established early, particularly during the first year of life. If the alcoholism in the child's family is not severe enough to preoccupy or control the parents (especially the mother), they may be emotionally available for their child. The more reliable and consistent they are emotionally, the more likely it is that the child will be able to develop a sense of trust in other people.

If, however, the alcoholism is severe enough to preoccupy, control, and drain the parents, they are less able to meet their child's emotional needs. This is when, we believe, the initial seed can be sown for developing an eating disorder.

Trust is built and maintained by proper feeding, consistent attention, physical contact, and love. Inconsistent care may increase a normal sense of loss as the child gradually recognizes her separateness from her mother. She may develop a basic mistrust that lasts throughout her life.

When the parents (especially the mother) see feeding the child as a nuisance, the child may associate food and eating with unpleasantness, anger, or disapproval. It is easy for the child to undereat to avoid those bad feelings.

On the other hand, if feeding time is the *only* time the child has emotional and physical contact with her parents (and particularly if feeding is consistent) we believe the child may easily begin to see eating as a way to get nurtured. Food can do more than ease her hunger pains.

Stage Two (2-3 Years Old)—Autonomy
Versus Shame and Doubt

Erikson viewed the quest for interdependence (balance of becoming independent with being able to accept and process feedback from others) as the next step of development. Erikson indicates that through this stage a child develops self-control. Here again, we believe that if the alcoholism is not controlling, preoccupying, and draining the parents, the child may be able to develop self-control and be open to others, which reduces her risk of developing an eating disorder. If, however, the disease of alcoholism has progressed to the point that the parents are using inconsistent methods of discipline, the child's susceptibility increases.

As the child asserts her independence, food can become a battleground between child and mother. As the alcoholic or codependent mother struggles with her own feelings of inadequacy, the one maternal task that makes her feel worthwhile is cooking and preparing meals. Making sure her child eats "properly" gives her a sense of success as a mother.

During this stage, all children try to exert their independence. Food can fuel the power struggle between mother and child. If food is a battleground, the child uses food to assert her independence. Depending on the mother's response and her feelings about food, her weight and her child's weight, she may try to lessen the child's sense of herself, which leads to intense feelings of shame and self-doubt. As this battle goes on, the child feels even more shameful and doubts herself. If a child eats unhealthy foods or overeats, the way a mother helps the child make choices and develop self-control can be a factor later on in compulsive eating patterns.

Self-control is part of developing a positive self-image. If her parents' drinking is out of control during this stage of the child's development, she is faced with a dilemma as she tries to develop self-control. First, there is no one in the family who can model self-control. Instead, she sees extremes. Someone is out of control (probably the alcoholic) and someone is overcontrolling (most likely the enabler). The child, therefore, sees self-control as an issue of extremes and begins modeling these behaviors.

The child doesn't see self-control as satisfying. Instead, she sees it as a period of intense restrictiveness and deprivation, followed by abandonment of responsible behavior. We, the authors, see this in all of our patients. The cycle of deprivation (starvation, dieting, excessive exercise, purging) followed by abandonment of responsible behavior (bingeing) falls neatly into the extremism of addictive illness.

Stage Three (4-5 Years Old)—Initiative Versus Guilt

This stage is characterized by a curiosity about the world and the need to explore this world. If her curiosity brings criticism or no response at all, the child's natural curiosity suffers. She may then experience a sense of guilt or failure.

An internal conflict in the alcoholic family also can begin at this stage. The child, as she explores her world, must learn to comply with the family's denial that the disease of alcoholism exists in the family. What she sees and feels is often not what she's told she sees and feels, creating distrust of her perceptions and feelings. Her conscience is developed during this stage, and if parents respond negatively to things their child attempts to understand, her guilt feelings increase.

In the alcoholic family, alcoholism is the center of attention. The child's initiative is often squelched, criticized, or ignored. The child gets no support or affirmation and she begins to feel as though she is bad. If the child isn't given credit for her efforts, she feels inferior. Her feelings of unworthiness and guilt may be eased by a cookie or ice cream. Her mother, trying to ease her guilt, may use food as a way to justify her lack of skill as a mother.

If Stage Two is still unresolved and the power struggle

with food continues, the youngster may use food to numb her uncomfortable feelings.

This sense of failure (even faced with success) is common in a patient with an eating disorder. She has not developed an internal measure of her accomplishments. Even though she may receive praise from others, her feelings of failure remain strong.

Stage Four (6-12 Years Old)—
Industry Versus Inferiority

This stage focuses on learning how to do and make things with others. A child wants to participate in the world, and school offers that opportunity. Nevertheless, a child's feelings of uselessness and inferiority can be carried into school. If she has learned that she's not useful at home, she carries that feeling with her into the classroom.

Parents who are focused on alcoholism aren't able to provide support or to guide their child educationally and socially at this stage. Success in school depends on how well the child has done in her earlier stages of development.

It's at school, however, that the child can be affirmed by teachers or peers, if she's intellectually or socially adept. She can get some of her needs met at school, but returning home each day fuels her feelings of guilt and inadequacy. If she can succeed at school, why can't she succeed at home? Her feelings of confusion and despair increase. Food can numb her negative feelings by providing a sense of nurturance and warmth.

If the child doesn't do well academically and socially in school, food can become a way out. It's one thing she has control over; it's one thing that makes her feel good without having to depend on anyone else. If she starts gaining weight, it can shield her from her feelings of inferiority. She begins to believe that her weight is the problem.

Stage Five (13-18 Years Old)—Identity Versus Diffusion

In this stage, as described by Erikson, the child attempts to answer the question, "Who am I?" A child who grows up in an alcoholic family isn't able to answer this. Her underlying feelings of shame, guilt, inadequacy, and inferiority make this a painful question for her to even try to answer. She still has unresolved conflicts from her earlier stages of development and is overinvolved with the nonalcoholic parent; this makes her out of touch with her internal self. Because of society's messages, girls have a harder time developing a sense of self than boys.

Often our eating disorder patients talk about using food to "fill a hole inside." Their lack of a sense of self creates an emptiness only food seems to fill. Many eating disorders begin during this stage of development. Adolescence can recap a child's earlier stages of life. If issues with food and eating weren't played out then, they will emerge now.

As the youngster matures, peer and cultural influences become increasingly important. For young girls, becoming a woman is frightening. There are so many choices, so much pressure to succeed. We have discussed the cultural pressures placed on all women and have noted in Chapter Two that eating disorders are becoming more prevalent because of the changing sex roles women face. These cultural pressures, plus family sex-role behaviors and attitudes can be fertile ground for developing an eating disorder.

In alcoholic families, the daughter is usually enmeshed with the enabler (the nonalcoholic parent) and feels no sense of self. She finds she can use food, weight, and dieting as a way to achieve her own identity. This is one area of her life that's under her control. Her eating disorder consumes her thinking, all her energies. It's her secret. Many women have great difficulty letting go of their eating disorders because they're unable to experience themselves in any other way. The eating disorder becomes the focus of their lives; without it they feel there is nothing. The vomiting or bingeing is a way to assert independence from family and, at the same time, express hostility.

Her relationship with food mirrors her love-hate relationship with her family, particularly her enabling mother. It mirrors her struggle between her dependency feelings that she sees as weak and powerless, and her need for independence, which she sees as powerful. She thinks in extremes. To her, all her feelings are weak; on the other hand, being in control and having no feelings is strong. Bingeing is her weakness, but dieting and purging is her strength.

Stage Six (19-25 Years Old)—Intimacy Versus Isolation

This stage is characterized by a person's ability or inability to develop intimate relationships. Fear of intimacy is a paramount struggle for ACOAs. It's also difficult for compulsive eaters.

Isolation is a symptom of an eating disorder. Many eating disorder patients isolate themselves from the rest of the world emotionally and physically. This isolation is usually based on distrust, fear of being hurt, and the fear of being "found out" as a terrible person.

Incomplete progression through the earlier stages can result in an internal struggle of wanting, yet fearing to be close to others. Without a sense of a self, it's difficult to allow another person to become close. Many eating disorder patients fear closeness because they're afraid of being consumed by the other person.

Rituals involving food and weight can replace companionship. Overweight patients often describe their weight as a way to protect themselves and keep others at a distance. For the bulimic, her secret and frequent feelings of disgust about her purging encourage her to be more careful about how close her relationships will be.

A summary of Erikson's six stages of emotional development is described in Chart Five.

CHART FIVE

Stages of Emotional Development

STAGE 1

to trust

1 year old

How consistent is feeding?

What is attitude of mother toward one-year-old child?

What is mother's attitude toward being a mother?

What is mother's attitude toward food for herself?

STAGE 2

to be independent

self-discipline

shame

2-3 years old

How are food choices for child handled?

Who makes decisions about what, when, and how much she eats?

How are internal feelings of hunger validated and by whom?

What is atmosphere of mealtimes?

Does food become a power struggle between mother and child?

STAGE 3

to explore

guilt

4-5 years old

Conscience begins to develop.

Food can begin to be used to sedate feelings of guilt, powerlessness.

STAGE 4

to be productive

inferiority

6-12 years old

Food is used to sedate feelings.

Females learn appearance is more important than accomplishments.

Pleasing others results in positive feedback.

Love/trust relationship with food becomes solidified.

STAGE 5

to become a person

nonperson

13-18 years old

Food, eating, weight become focus of self.

Food is what can be controlled with no interference.

STAGE 6

to discover

intimacy

isolation

19-25 years old

Isolation continues with increased emphasis on weight, food, eating.

Feelings of powerlessness and hopelessness increase

Do Parents Follow
Traditional Sex-Role Behaviors?

Changing Sex Roles

Sex-roles can be defined as those learned behaviors and attitudes that are assumed to be characteristic of an individual based on stereotypes accepted by society.

Our culture expects men to be strong, reliable, forceful, aggressive, athletic, competitive, ambitious, and analytical. Women, on the other hand, are seen as passive, submissive, nurturing, compassionate, tender, helpful, unpredictable, sensitive to others' needs, and sacrificing.

Women have another important ideal to conform to: *the perfect body.* And that body is defined by our culture. For centuries, women have been socialized to be dissatisfied with their bodies. Nearly every civilization imposes an ideal shape upon the feminine body that rearranges, accentuates, or dramatically reduces some part of the female anatomy.

Sex-Role Conflict/Body Image Conflict

In the last 20 years, men and women have seen a shift in their sex-roles. For example, a generation ago it was unusual for a man to go grocery shopping, diaper a baby, hug another man, cry in public, cook and sew, or take care of a sick child. It was unusual then for a woman to pursue a career, pay alimony, be sexually aggressive, choose not to have children, be athletic, make more money than her spouse, or give up custody of her children.

In addition to these role changes, our culture's ideal female body has changed. Research conducted over a 20 year span shows a dramatic shift toward thinness as a feminine quality.

Even though these changes have swept over men and women, accepting them happens slowly. Many men and women feel confused and uncertain about how they should behave and feel; consequently they experience sex-role conflict. For women, this conflict includes her body image. They're uncertain about how to behave and feel, and they have negative feelings toward their bodies, ranging from mild discomfort to extreme loathing.

Sex-role conflict results from confusion about what's learned and what we're supposed to feel or do because of our sex, instead of what we'd like to do or feel. For example, a woman may experience sex-role conflict if she believes a woman's primary role is to have children, but she does not want children.

A person who experiences body image conflict is never satisfied with her body and has a distorted picture of her body in her mind. For example, in the extreme, the anorexic who is emaciated *feels* fat. So does the bulimic, who may be average weight. An obese person denies and minimizes her weight. Neither of them has an accurate perception of her size.

Although society's attitude toward men's and women's roles has changed, most of us still struggle with the beliefs and attitudes we grew up with. Traditional sex-role attitudes are deeply engrained. Changing these attitudes so we can become more whole and integrated is a slow and painful process. It's a process that requires people, regardless of their sex, to take full responsibility for the quality of their lives (physical and emotional), for getting their needs met, and for realizing their full potential.

Unspoken Expectations

Some men aren't taught how to take care of their emotional needs. They've been taught to minimize their emotional needs and to expect their emotional needs to be taken care of by women. They depend on women to know what their unspoken emotional and physical needs are. They expect this to happen as long as they're good providers, self-sufficient, and able to take care of the "weaker" sex.

Some women, too, aren't taught how to take care of their emotional needs. They're often socialized to be responsible for the emotional and physical needs of the family. They're also often expected to take care of their own emotional needs. Women are taught to believe that if they're attractive, good at taking care of others, kind, loving, self-sacrificing, and nurturing, they can expect to have their emotional and physical needs met. In this type of environment, their expectations are rarely discussed, but seem to be based on the assumption that men's needs are the same and that they each are responsible for the other—he for providing, she for nurturing.

Consequently, in this way both women and men learn to not be responsible for their feelings and needs and learn to never discuss or acknowledge that they want, feel, or need anything.

Some women are encouraged to not put themselves first, to anticipate others' needs, and to seek a sense of self through their relationships. Because of this, women often deny themselves and are unable to define their needs or to admit they have needs and desires. Because they're so preoccupied with others, they depend on the approval of others. This fosters insecurity, a shaky sense of self, or a feeling of emptiness. This feeling of emptiness can become one of several warning signs of the onset of an eating disorder.

The Alcoholic Family Following Traditional Sex Roles

Mom's and Dad's relationship, their behaviors, values, and verbal messages all influence their child's sense of identity, competency, power, and worth as a male or as a female. (Of course, a child's peers, teachers, television, magazines, and society at large also influence her feelings about what is appropriate as her world expands.) Many studies indicate that alcoholic families cling to traditional roles. Chemically dependent couples tend to see things in extremes or in black-and-white terms, making it easy to follow traditional male and female roles.

Women are expected to be both dependent and everyone's emotional caretakers, but not to express their own emotional needs. Men are supposed to be taken care of emotionally by women, without it ever being acknowledged. If either person acknowledges his or her needs and takes responsibility for meeting them, the power balance in the relationship would be shaken. The male would have to acknowledge his feminine side, and the female would have to acknowledge her masculine side.

The old sex-role definitions were based on a division of labor. He went to work and was responsible for economic survival; she stayed at home and was responsible for domestic survival. He was head of the household; she let him make family decisions. The roles became more important than people.

Alcoholism protects and supports traditional roles. For the male alcoholic, drinking may make a man feel masculine, while letting him be emotionally dependent. It encourages him to be emotionally underresponsible and, at the same time, keeps the illusion that he's the head of the household. While drinking, the male alcoholic is freed to express his "feminine" side; he can be emotional, sensitive, and irrational. It provides a "masculine" way to express his feminine side.

As he continues drinking, he makes fewer decisions. The female becomes more responsible. She handles more and more of the family responsibilities, expressing her masculine side while at the same time maintaining the facade of being feminine.

They both blame their opposite sex behaviors on the alcohol. The alcohol prevents them from questioning the power balance in the relationship. Let's look at this relationship more closely as it's played out in the family.

The codependent wife must maintain the illusion that the family is normal—the family is a reflection of her success as a woman. As the alcoholic husband becomes less involved in the family, she becomes more responsible and an enabler. She can't let the family fall apart, but she can't let anyone outside the family know how much she's doing. She feels self-doubt, fear, self-hate, and anger because of the deception. She knows she's lying to herself, to her family, and to the world. She must also deal with her constant fear of being found out. She's angry with her self and with her spouse for being in this situation, yet she feels paralyzed and unable to do anything about it.

She resents being forced to be responsible, because of the emotional pressures to do everything and because it calls her femininity into question. If she's bought the idea that being feminine means being taken care of, dependent, loving, and kind, and if she's required to be independent, aggressive, and a decision-maker, she can't help but question her femininity. Often, her self-doubt is made more painful by her alcoholic husband who verbalizes her inner doubts.

The alcoholic's guilt, self-hatred, and questioning of his masculinity (through his steady loss of control as the disease progresses) keeps him caught in the drinking cycle. Overwhelmed by his feelings, he often projects his feelings onto his spouse. He does this by becoming very critical, particularly of her femininity. He criticizes and questions her appearance, her sexuality, and her homemaking skills. He's trying to reestablish his self-esteem, masculinity, and leadership in the family. By listening to and internalizing his criticisms, she subconsciously tries to keep her traditional role of dependency and helplessness.

A young girl growing up in this family is often told her father is the provider and head of the household, but she sees her mother as the one who holds everything together, controls who does what, and makes all the decisions. But, if mother has so much power and control, why does she put up with his drinking? Why doesn't she leave? What is she afraid of? This creates real confusion for the daughter. She doesn't realize the alcoholism gives her mother power. It's not real power, but she sees her mother's masculine side emerge as a result.

As the daughter observes her parents, she feels her mother's internal conflict and she struggles to understand what's happening. How can her mother be so strong yet so weak and not leave him? How can her father be so strong and yet so weak that he can't stop drinking? She observes extreme sex-role behaviors from both of her parents.

While the family focuses on maintaining the dysfunctional system, the youngster finds food has magical qualities. It starts when she feels anxiety about her parents arguing. She picks up a few cookies and her uncomfortable feelings seem to disappear. She feels much better than she did before. These good feelings reinforce her relationship to food. A love-trust relationship is established; food makes her feel safe and secure. It becomes her companion, the one thing she can trust to always make her feel better.

But something else begins to happen: people start commenting about her weight or she finds her clothes are too tight. She panics. She then diets, fasts, and exercises to regain control and lose weight. This begins to change her body. When a person diets, the body adjusts to a lower caloric intake, the metabolic rate slows down, and it becomes easier to gain weight. So the more times a person diets, the harder it becomes to lose weight. Her anxiety about the weight gain fuels her purging behavior. What originally felt good has now taken on a life of its own.

This cycle begins to create feelings of control and power within her. Her bingeing is her "feminine," out of control, weak, helpless side. But her dieting, fasting, or purging is her "masculine," independent, aggressive, in control side. Just like her mother and father, she plays out her sex-role conflict with a substance.

The only thing she feels she can control is her paradoxical relationship with food. Her eating disorder becomes the core of her identity.

The pain of her dysfunctional family life, her parents' relationship, and her relationship with each of them becomes unbearable. As most children do, she feels responsible and that there must be something wrong with her.

She has all these feelings she doesn't understand; but she does understand her relationship with food. And deep down she knows this isn't normal.

While life at home becomes more chaotic, she begins school and develops peer relationships. She is exposed to the world's expectations of her as a female. She sees billboards and magazine ads that show women as thin and beautiful. Thin symbolizes being in control and being powerful. Thin will make her unlike her mother who has an unhappy life and who may be overweight and a compulsive eater herself. Or her mother may be extremely weight conscious and able to control her eating, unlike her father who can't control his drinking.

She begins to understand what she should be like if she's going to succeed as a woman—she must be thin. This desire to be thin puts her relationship with food in jeopardy. But she knows she can have the best of both worlds by bingeing and then purging or dieting.

The obsession with thinness is her addiction and, like all addictions, it keeps her alienated from herself. As she continues her addictive relationship with food, she becomes more depressed and consumed with self-hate. Just like her mother, she knows power comes from a substance. She doesn't develop a sense of competence, self-worth, and real power because she hasn't accepted herself.

As we mentioned earlier, the more common family background in the development of an eating disorder relates to the female children with Dad as the alcoholic. When the mother is the drinker, sex-role issues are equally evident. For women, however, there is the added burden of the stigma associated with engaging in such "unladylike" behavior. The effects on the sex-role development of the daughter are equally confusing.

The child growing up in an alcoholic family system cannot know that Dad's drinking is one way Dad can feel masculine and emotional at the same time. She cannot know that Dad's drinking gives Mom the opportunity to be powerful and in control while maintaining her role as a passive, accepting, and submissive female. A daughter can't know because her parents don't know. The whole system is shortsighted and unrealistic, and it makes everyone question his or her identity and normalcy.

The Family's Value on Food and Weight

We believe that the family's values about food and weight strongly influence the child of an alcoholic family. She is much more likely to develop an eating disorder.

We have already discussed how important appearances are in an alcoholic family. This emphasis on appearances often includes the weight of the family members, particularly the female members. A normal desire to look good can become an obsession for the alcoholic family as they strive to measure up to ideal images and to appear normal to the outside world.

Often, ACOAs reveal that one or both of their parents were overweight or were compulsive (in some way) about eating. More often than not, the mother had rigid attitudes about food and weight or compulsively ate. This isn't surprising given the cultural pressures women feel to be thin.

As the alcoholic becomes more dependent on alcohol, the enabler becomes more dependent on appearances: doing things right, having children who do well and look good become her focus. As her feelings of emptiness increase, however, she realizes that appearances aren't enough to make her feel better and that she doesn't have any control over the alcoholic or the chaotic family.

Fear that stems from a belief that everything in life could become a disaster may push her to use something concrete to create a false sense of security. That's when she's likely to turn to food and compulsive eating to express, sedate, and deny her pain.

When Mom uses food and gains weight, Dad often becomes critical, particularly if she's critical of his drinking. The female children see this and make a connection between weight, worthiness, and acceptance.

If being thin is valued by Mom or Dad, the daughter may become obsessed with her weight. This may be especially true if the alcoholic father values thinness. His daughter may see being thin as a way to get emotionally close to her father.

Some women, particularly mothers, have often measured their personal adequacy in the preparation of food, the types and amounts of food their children will eat, and the visible results (fitness, weight, and physical health) of their families. Through the years, some women have used food to bolster their self-esteem and personal power. Think of all the old sayings that tell women how their abilities with food determine their acceptability:

"A way to a man's heart is through his stomach."

"A fat baby is a healthy, happy baby."

These statements tell women, "If you don't value and know what you're doing with food you're going to end up alone, unloved, and a failure."

Women have been told to use food to manipulate others into approving of and feeling close to them. The enabling mother may try to make things normal by preparing a lot of food and insisting the family eat together. She may use food to foster closeness with her children. Fixing special treats or going out together for desserts or special meals is her way of being special to her children. Given her low self-esteem, she may believe that she can get her children to love her more if she gives them more nurturing and love through food. At the other end of the spectrum, going to diet clubs or going on diets together is a way to foster closeness between Mom and her overweight child.

If she gets angry enough, Mother can use food to punish other family members. She may stop cooking and have a "let them fend for themselves" attitude. This usually happens in later stages of alcoholism, when the mother's emotional resources are nearly tapped dry.

A mother may also use food to make up for the alcoholic's absence or insensitivity. When Dad doesn't show up for the promised trip to the zoo, Mom may compensate by fixing a special treat or taking her daughter out for a pizza. The message is "Food will make you feel loved, will make you feel better."

If the daughter's appearance is a way to obtain affirmation from the alcoholic parent, the child will begin to struggle with the crisis of "losing" by attempting to satisfy both parents. It is likely a young woman will diet or lose weight to gain attention and approval from an alcoholic father who values thinness in women. If, however, her mother sees the weight loss as a threat to her control of her daughter, she may send a message of disappointment, hurt, or disapproval. Since children in alcoholic families anticipate the needs, feelings, and desires of others, they pick up on this disapproval. The daughter may then feel compelled to abandon her efforts to be thin. If she then gains weight and is criticized for it by her alcoholic parent, the child may face the onset of a yo-yo weight syndrome, which emotionally and biologically sets her up for a lifelong struggle with food and weight.

At puberty, the daughter of an alcoholic family, which has valued and used food as described above, gets mixed messages and mixed emotions from her family and the culture. Also, her mind and body begin to act and respond in new ways.

Puberty and sexuality are a central, vital part of being an adolescent. It's a time when a teenager develops a new awareness of her body. Psychologically, an adolescent experiences all things more intensely. Sexual feelings can make a teenager have guilt feelings. With time, her guilt feelings will diminish unless she's living in an alcoholic family. In that case, they will persist and may intensify. The daughter may try to repress her confusion by desexualizing herself by excessive weight loss or weight gain.

Entering adolescence, a daughter needs reassurance and approval from her parents before she can become part of a peer culture. The confusion of the alcoholic family doesn't create the environment necessary for the daughter to obtain the approval and reassurance she needs. The actions of the mother and father of the daughter who develops an eating disorder block any efforts by the daughter to take the steps necessary to "grow up" both physically and emotionally. Alcoholic families are rigid and filled with fear, making it hard to accept normal life cycle changes. Children entering adolescence are a threat to the delicate balance of denial because puberty and adolescence is a major transitional cycle that's virtually impossible to ignore.

If Mother is overweight, she's likely to do one of two things. She may directly encourage her daughter to "be like me" and foster compulsive eating behaviors that result in her daughter being overweight. Or she will directly tell her daughter, "Don't be like me; don't be overweight," but then sabotage her daughter's efforts to maintain a healthy weight and to have a separate personal life. In this case, the message the daughter receives is "Grow up! Be independent! Be your own person, but don't get too fat. Don't leave me behind!"

When Dad gets involved, he adds to the confusion. He either lashes out at his daughter for being "just like your mother," or he supports her for being different from her mother if she's thin and Mom is overweight.

Levels of Emotional Involvement in the Family System

One factor we believe to influence the ACOA's development of an eating disorder is the level of emotional involvement she has within the alcoholic family system. The degree of this involvement controls the intensity and type of emotional bond she has with the alcoholic and the enabling spouse.

In our clinical experience our patients have reported two levels of emotional involvement they experienced when growing up in their dysfunctional families. We have labeled these levels of emotional involvement as *triangulation* and *disengagement.*

Triangulation occurs when the child is overly involved with the marital pair. This overinvolvement can be positive or negative.

For purposes of clarity, we will call a positively triangulated child the *Banner Carrier.* She will receive attention and an emotional and behavioral response from her parents that is unhealthy, but still affirming.

A negatively triangulated child is the *Troublemaker.* She will receive attention and an emotional and behavioral response from her parents that is negative, often hostile, and demeaning.

Disengagement occurs when the child is underinvolved with either parent. This underinvolvement can be positive or negative.

A positively disengaged child is what we'll call the

Clown. She gets needs met at a superficial level and receives minimal positive attention from her parents.

A negatively disengaged child is the *Invisible Child.* She also gets minimal attention from her parents, but this attention lacks any emotional substance. Consequently, she gets few, if any, other emotional needs met.

In our treatment experience, we have found that the Banner Carrier and the Invisible Child are most likely to develop an eating disorder. Nevertheless, we do not believe this excludes the Troublemaker or the Clown from being susceptible to developing an eating disorder.

We will discuss each level of involvement and how it promotes problems with compulsive eating in the ACOA.

The Banner Carrier

This is often the oldest child, or the oldest child of each gender, or the oldest child in each "family" if the children are significantly spread out chronologically. Or she may be the child who, in her personal growth, is the oldest one still emotionally tied to both parents—particularly the nonalcoholic parent.

The Banner Carrier's banner states "This family is normal, happy, and successful." She always does what's right and what's expected to live out the myth that the family is normal. She is overly responsible for the feelings and needs of others. She needs everyone's approval because that's the only way she knows if she's carrying the banner high enough.

Her job is to make Mom and Dad feel better about themselves. She does this by making up for their weaknesses and keeping Mom and Dad together. She is emotionally bonded to both parents. Nevertheless, this may not be seen in her relationship with her mother, the enabler. The visible alliance between the enabler and the Banner Carrier becomes more apparent as the alcoholic's emotional and physical isolation increases. She becomes more and more dependent on the enabler as a role model. This means she sees manipulation, passive-aggressive anger, deception, the need to be in control, overextending herself, guilt, self-hate, and a sense of inadequacy as normal and unavoidable.

The daughter playing the role of the Banner Carrier is enmeshed, particularly with her mother. Being enmeshed is not having any identity or sense of self. Instead, personal identity and self-worth depends on how others treat you and how well you live up to other people's expectations.

The Banner Carrier feels it's her responsibility to take care of her parents—especially her mother. She hopes that she'll receive approval, unconditional love and acceptance, and her own needs will be met. This rarely happens.

Because the mother is so caught up in the alcoholism, she can't give her daughter the ongoing approval, love, and acceptance she desperately wants. She can't help her daughter learn how to get personal needs met because, as a codependent, she can't identify or meet her own needs. Instead, the mother places more demands and expectations on her daughter. In response, the Banner Carrier continues to try to fulfill these demands, this time hoping approval, acceptance, and love will be there. This is how the vicious cycle of perfectionism, people-pleasing, and inadequacy begins and escalates.

Achievement is important to the Banner Carrier. This achievement is measured through external things—good grades, involvement in the right social groups, being mature for her age, being mother's confidante, and a second mom to younger siblings.

At one time, she may have been expected to be a good caretaker. With the sex role revolution, however, the adult Banner Carrier must also be successful in the work world. The Banner Carrier of today is constantly experiencing confusion and chaos. In her efforts to be all things to all people there is little reward. Her sense of identity is constantly questioned because she has never quite measured up. Nothing she does is ever good enough, at least not for very long. Her path to love, acceptance, and approval has become a path filled with pain, inadequacy, and anger.

As she becomes more and more addicted to perfection, she becomes less and less in touch with herself. Her internal void, often described by a compulsive eater as a "hole inside," becomes bigger. Compulsive eating is a way to fill the void, at least temporarily. It's also a way for her to feel she has control over something. As home becomes more and more chaotic, she may become preoccupied with food, weight, and calories. She tells herself, if only I were thinner, I'd be happy and successful. Focusing on getting, being, or staying thin lets the Banner Carrier deny the real causes of her pain and anger.

She sees being thin as being in control and being overweight as being out of control. This turmoil reflects her feelings about her family role. Because she's so essential to the balance of the family system, she can't develop an identity apart from that system. Doing so, she believes, would be a betrayal.

Whether she is purging or gaining weight, the Banner Carrier who is a compulsive eater tries to define herself apart from her role in the family system. At the same time, however, she's driven to keep the family together. Bingeing is a way to lessen her conflict over meeting her own needs versus meeting the needs of her family or her mother.

Consequently, the eating disorder is a way for her to have an identity apart from the family without threatening its delicate balance. Her identity gives her the freedom to be imperfect. She can continue to please others, achieve, and try to ease the family's pain, but she can also be angry and rebel through her bingeing and purging behavior.

For the Banner Carrier, compulsive eating is a way to express her fears while maintaining her role (which through the years has become her whole identity) and protecting her family system.

The Invisible Child

The Invisible Child is also highly susceptible to developing an eating disorder because she has no way to gain attention or to get her needs met in her family. She isn't emotionally close to anyone. Confused by the chaos of the family, she retreats and isolates herself. She's forced by the alcoholic family to find a way to feel better all by herself.

If the alcoholism is severe in the early years of her life (ages three to ten) this isolation could lead to imaginary friends, a vivid fantasy world, daydreaming, and wishful thinking. It can also lead to compulsive eating. After all, food is readily available to her, and is something she can get for herself. Food becomes a friend and confidante. It gives her a false sense of being nurtured. Consequently, she doesn't develop early social skills with either her family or playmates. This becomes more extreme as she moves into adolescence. She doesn't know how to develop relationships, and it's likely that her compulsive use of food will increase as she gets older. Being with people and being in intimate relationships become a burden for her; she feels awkward and self-conscious. Her eating soothes her, and her weight protects her from a threatening environment.

The Invisible Child is usually overweight. Her weight acts like a cocoon protecting her from a world and people she doesn't feel equipped to deal with. At a deeper level, she doesn't wish to call attention to herself by being thin. In the early stages of her disease, food is the one thing she can count on to always be there.

The Troublemaker

We rarely see an adult child in the role of Troublemaker who's a compulsive eater. We are not sure why. One reason might be that this child is more likely to act out by becoming chemically dependent, promiscuous, or a delinquent. These acting out behaviors are usually done within her peer group. Consequently, the Troublemaker expresses her anger and pain through covert activities within the peer culture. These activities are rarely as unobtrusive and isolated as over- or undereating.

Traditional male and female behaviors are fostered in the alcoholic family, and Troublemakers, who are usually aggressive, tend to be boys. Girls are encouraged to be submissive and compliant; these behaviors are more consistent with the dynamics of an eating disorder. However, both male and female Troublemakers tend to be runaways and academic underachievers. They are more likely to drink and use other drugs and be sexually promiscuous. Teenage pregnancies are common in this group. These behaviors illustrate the rage the Troublemaker feels.

The Banner Carrier, who attempts to win her parents' unconditional love, acceptance, and approval by taking care of them, feels the same intense rage, except she turns it inward. This is also true for the Invisible Child. The Troublemaker, however, attempts to find love, acceptance, and approval from peer group members who are often just as troubled and needy. These relationships are often shallow and based on exploitation and manipulation. Consequently, the Troublemaker feels unacceptable and unloved.

Given the Troublemaker's low self-esteem, drugs ease the pain better than food. An eating disorder is a passive way of expressing anger, much too subdued for the attention-getting tactics of the Troublemaker.

We do see the female Troublemaker as likely to develop an eating disorder if her boyfriend or peer group friends are concerned with weight. A Troublemaker whose boyfriend thinks she's too fat may diet strictly, fearing she'll lose her primary source of love and affection if she isn't thin enough.

If her peer group is weight conscious and involved in bulimic behaviors, she may participate in these behaviors as a way to belong. The difference between the Banner Carrier and the Troublemaker is in who the person is trying to please and feel accepted by. The rage and the low self-esteem are similar for both.

The Clown

Traditionally, the Clown is the youngest child in the family. Nevertheless, any child that the alcoholic family overprotects (the only daughter or son, or a child with a handicap) can be the Clown. Like all other children in an alcoholic family, the Clown feels her parents are emotionally unavailable.

She feels alone, confused, and out of control. We have rarely seen a Clown who becomes dependent on food and weight as a way to get her needs met. By nature, she has her comic antics to do these things for her.

In order to get attention, she resorts to clowning or joking. This constant struggle to relieve tension in the family keeps the Clown immature and childlike. Consequently, she is limited in being able to function as an adult.

Unlike the Banner Carrier, the Troublemaker, and the Invisible Child, who live an existence based on anger, the Clown lives an existence based on fear—fear that her whole world could collapse at any moment. The laughter, the jokes, and the clowning are diversionary tactics that temporarily help her feel in control.

As she gets older, her cuteness becomes something to laugh at, but it's her ticket into relationships (even though these are superficial). The attention her humor brings her becomes as addictive as alcohol or food. Without it, she feels empty, like a failure.

As the Clown moves into adulthood, she's unable to meet the expectations of others and is confused as to the parameters of these expectations. The internal stress this creates for her (particularly since the Clown isn't able to act responsibly), can result in her using food to cope, but more often results in chemical dependency or psychiatric illness. Food doesn't meet the all-powerful need for attention the Clown craves.

For the Clown daughter whose role may take on more of the aspects of being cute or funny rather than hyperactive, clumsy, or irresponsible, weight may be used to physically validate her role. For example, she may starve herself to stay a little girl or she may overeat and gain weight, remaining asexual or "fat and jolly."

Characteristics
of Alcoholic Family Roles
and Eating Disorders

ACOA/Compulsive Eater Banner Carrier
- anger turned inward
- focus on parents to get needs met
- enmeshed in parents' relationship

ACOA/Compulsive Eater Invisible Child
- anger turned inward
- isolates
- focus on self to get needs met

ACOA/Compulsive Eater Troublemaker
- anger turned outward
- focus on peer group to get needs met

ACOA/Compulsive Eater Clown
- anger repressed
- focus on others to get needs met

Some ACOAs who compulsively eat have a combination of role characteristics, such as Banner Carrier and Clown as well as Invisible Child and Clown.

CHAPTER
- 4 -

Treatment for the ACOA
Who is a Compulsive Eater

ACOAs who are compulsive eaters need to realize they have a disease that's similar to alcoholism. Just like chemical dependency, food addiction carries with it a great deal of denial. The compulsive eater's denial is reinforced by our culture which promotes diets and quick weight-loss schemes. It tells people they can buy control. The compulsive eater has established an identity that says, "I am not a compulsive eater and I am in control." This identity perpetuates the bingeing and feelings of depression, self-hate, and powerlessness.

Instead of worrying about control, a sound recovery program provides structure for a recovering person. Unlike diets, which are seen as an event, a recovery program for compulsive eating is lifelong and focuses on altering a person's relationship with food. Once this relationship is more manageable, the recovering person can begin to work on issues that deal with interpersonal relationships, self-esteem, and spirituality.

In early recovery, the compulsive eater needs to make a shift in her identity. She must move from "I can control what I eat. I am not a compulsive eater" to "I cannot control what I eat. I am a compulsive eater." By admitting powerlessness, the compulsive eater gains control by managing her relationship with food. She moves from searching for an external means of control (diets) to an internal means of control (following a recovery program). A program of lifelong recovery is needed to manage the disease. This program should include the following elements:

- learn about and work the Twelve Steps as they relate to compulsive eating;
- develop a sound abstinence concept (abstinence from compulsive eating);
- develop a flexible food and exercise plan;
- attend Twelve Step support groups, including Adult Children of Alcoholics and Overeaters Anonymous meetings; and
- understand that relapse is a part of the disease.

Let's examine each area more fully.

Learn about and work the Twelve Steps as they relate to compulsive eating. The Twelve Steps promote behavioral change to help addicted individuals live a meaningful life. The Steps are the foundation for any recovery program.

We've found that compulsive eaters have a difficult time admitting they are powerless over their addiction to food. Food is what sustains life; without it we die. Our culture continually reinforces the belief that we can buy control, especially when it comes to eating. Dieting is a twenty billion dollar industry. This cultural brainwashing helps people deny their disease.

Although our culture encourages drinking, the pressure to eat and to celebrate with food is stronger and more common. Food is equated with love and caring; alcohol is not. Food preparation can be a labor of love. People who prepare meals feel a sense of failure if guests refuse to eat any particular food; it's seen almost as a personal rejection.

Develop a sound abstinence concept. Abstinence for the compulsive eater is complicated. A person can't stop eating. The goal of recovery is to change the relationship with food, to learn to live with the food. Chemically dependent people, on the other hand, must divorce themselves from drugs and learn to live without them.

Abstinence for the compulsive eater consists of three components:

1. *Physical.* This includes a food and exercise plan which limits high-fat foods and sugar and refined carbohydrates—known binge foods. It involves abstinence from the following: dieting, weighing oneself, eating between meals, a sedentary lifestyle, and counting calories.

2. *Emotional.* This includes abstinence from: negative self-talk, negative thoughts about oneself, pleasing others at the expense of personal needs and feelings, shutting off feelings, isolating oneself, or participating in relationships that diminish self-worth.

3. *Spiritual.* This means living life according to a thoughtful personal value system. Developing spirituality involves refraining from the belief that all things in life must be dealt with alone. It includes developing a relationship with a Higher Power, letting go of control, and realizing that being in control does not guarantee freedom from safety and hurt.

Compulsive eaters must learn to develop a concept of abstinence as a part of their recovery that is *workable,* not ideal. Physical abstinence is a controversial aspect of recovery. Some people believe that compulsive eaters need to abstain from refined sugar and carbohydrates. This makes abstinence simple but dangerous. Research indicates that the more a person restricts specific foods from her diet, the more likely she'll be to crave that food. Eventually, she'll give in to those cravings. Several studies have found a link between restraint and binge eating. Food restriction may lead to bingeing.

Simply abstaining from sugars and refined carbohydrates doesn't help the compulsive eater develop a normal relationship with food. It keeps the compulsive eater feeling deprived—a dangerous feeling in any relationship, particularly with food. It often keeps them obsessed about what they can't have.

Develop a flexible food and exercise plan. Compulsive eaters need to develop a food and exercise plan as part of their abstinence program. This food and exercise plan needs to be flexible and changeable. Rigid food plans are diets in disguise.

Attend Twelve Step support groups, including Adult Children of Alcoholics and Overeaters Anonymous (O.A.) meetings. ACOAs need to deal with their adult children issues. The most effective way to do this is to participate in ACOA groups. Sharing feelings and experiences is a vital part of the healing process. Participating in O.A. groups will be a source of strength and support in the disease. These groups provide two necessary elements to a recovery program:

- they keep the overeater in touch with her disease; she can continue to hear about the disease and continue to share her struggles with the disease; and
- they allow the overeater to seek support from others and give voice to her feelings. Addictive illnesses keep one isolated and in denial about what is felt. Support groups are a tremendous aid in this respect.

Understand relapse in the disease process. This is a very critical issue for compulsive eaters. Compulsive eaters are prone to perfectionism; they equate what they put in their mouths with their self-worth. Any deviation from their goal results in feelings of worthlessness and despair. These feelings always lead to binge behavior. One binge equals failure for recovering compulsive eaters. Their tendency is to bounce back and go on a diet rather than return to the basics of their recovery program. Support groups are an excellent way to come to terms with this element of the disease.

Recovery Program

TWELVE STEPS
provides structure and foundation of behavioral
changes
deals with surrender versus control and denial
introduces concept of spirituality versus isolation
helping others
making amends

ABSTINENCE
clarifies how one will manage her disease
physically
emotionally
spiritually

FOOD AND EXERCISE PLAN
structures eating
reduces anxiety
management strategy to alter relationship with
food

TWELVE STEP MEETINGS
decreases isolation
increases bonding with others
keeps disease a reality

CHAPTER
-5-

Virge's Story

When Virge (five-foot-five) came into treatment, she weighed 210 pounds. Her weight had been as high as 280 and as low as 140. She had been involved in Overeaters Anonymous on and off and was currently participating in several O.A. groups. She was following an O.A. food plan, which she said led to her recent weight loss.

In spite of her success at dropping 40 pounds, Virge realized this would be temporary. She'd been successful at weight loss before but would eventually gain the weight back and would end up weighing more than she did before the diet.

She knew her struggle with weight was not normal. She knew her eating patterns were bizarre but she didn't know how to change them. She wanted to be successful at taking off weight and keeping it off. She was so sick and tired of being sick and tired—it was this desperation that pushed her into treatment.

The first time I saw her, she looked much older than her 34 years. Her clothing had no style or color. She walked with stooped shoulders and, from a distance, she looked arthritic. However, upon closer scrutiny her face looked more like that of a twenty year old. She had a clear complexion, deep brown eyes with a bit of the devil in them, a broad smile that revealed perfect white teeth, and curly blonde hair.

What was most striking about her was her deep, guttural laugh—and she laughed a lot. She was witty and had a knack for making a joke out of most anything. Most of her humor was directed at herself, particularly her weight.

As she came into my office the first time, she shook my hand and with a sheepish grin asked, "Do you think your couch can handle me?" Behind that smile and the twinkling eyes was a look of fear, the real fear of wondering if my furniture would hold someone her size. And even deeper than that fear, I sensed that she wondered if I could handle someone her size. I could feel her sense of shame.

As I reached out and put my arm around her shoulder to escort her into my office, I felt her body tighten and her eyes became downcast. I assured her that she would find my furniture most comfortable. As she sank into the sofa, she suddenly looked like a frightened child, and she began to weep.

In our first session, Virge intermittently talked and cried. She discussed her relationship with her mother, and most of our early sessions focused on their relationship.

As treatment progressed, Virge began to talk more and more about her father. She eventually admitted he was an alcoholic. Virge's body would become particularly tight when she discussed her relationship with her father. Her jaws and hands would clench, and she'd periodically pound the arm of the sofa.

Virge's earliest childhood recollection of her father was one in which he was drunk and verbally abusing her mother. She described the feelings of terror she had. Her mother would plead with him to leave her alone. He would just yell louder and would often hit Virge's mother. Sometimes, Virge would get caught in the crossfire and be struck.

Virge said these scenes became common, and each time

the fighting started she would experience a feeling of dread in the pit of her stomach. These verbal battles usually occurred at night, so the next day Virge would tiptoe around the house amidst the clutter of beer bottles, overloaded ashtrays, and glasses, and straighten up quietly. As the house began to stir, and Mom and Dad would rise to start the day, they both would act as though nothing had happened the night before. At first, this utterly amazed Virge. She could not understand how they could act like nothing happened. Life just went on. For a long time, she sometimes thought she imagined the whole thing.

When Virge questioned her mother about these nighttime battles, her mother would tell her she was making a mountain out of a molehill. Her dad had a little too much to drink, and everything was fine. Mom would tell her to be a good girl and clean the rest of the house. She also told her that she would take her out for some ice cream if she did a good job.

Even now, she was confused about what had really been going on. Through therapy, she began to realize that her mother's message was, you'll be rewarded if you don't make waves. If Virge cleaned the house and pretended everything was all right, she and Mom would go out for sundaes. Of course, these were fun times for her and eased Virge's fear that her family was falling apart. Virge cleaned the house well and learned quickly to pretend nothing was wrong. She began to keep her thoughts and feelings to herself.

She also remembered that her mom was weight conscious. When they would go out for ice cream (and they did this often), Mom always commented on how fattening it was. She told Virge how chubby Virge's grandmother was and that if she wasn't careful, she would be overweight.

Though Virge's grandmother had died before she was born, Virge saw pictures of her and didn't think she looked bad. As a matter of fact, she didn't think her mother needed to worry about her weight. She thought her mother was just perfect—she was the most beautiful woman she had ever seen.

Virge's dad didn't agree. Virge recalled that, sober or drunk, her father would criticize her mother, especially her appearance. When drunk, he always commented on how fat she was getting and said if she got too fat, he would leave her and Virge. Even when sober, he was never satisfied. If he wasn't criticizing her mother about her weight, it was about her hair or her clothes.

When Virge would get angry and try to defend her mother, her mom would tell her to go play. Virge remembers hating her father for being mean to her mom, and she also remembers being confused by her mother's acceptance of this criticism. Virge began to doubt her own thoughts and feelings.

Virge remembers her first binge episode vividly. She was eight years old, and it was during one of her parents' fights. Her dad was drunk, and he was being particularly verbally abusive to her mom. Mom's response was to tell Virge to go into the kitchen and do the dishes. Virge remembers feeling so angry that, as she was cleaning the kitchen, she began to cry. She felt alone and frightened at the intensity of her rage. There was always ice cream in the freezer so she decided to have some. While she was eating it, she felt the wave of rage disappear. The texture of the ice cream felt creamy and cold on her tongue. The next thing she knew, she had eaten the entire gallon. She was shocked to discover that it could all go down so easily. One thing was clear to her: she felt better.

With time, bingeing became easier and easier. Whether her parents were fighting or not, eating became the primary focus in Virge's life. She began associating food with being cared for and as a way to make uncomfortable feelings go away. Then something began to happen that

Virge didn't count on. At age twelve, she began to gain weight.

Both Virge's dad and mom began to comment on how fat she was getting. When her dad would criticize her weight, her mom would defend her and yell at her dad for being so insensitive. But, when her dad wasn't around, her mom would suggest that Virge go on a diet.

As the criticism increased, so did Virge's bingeing. She would sneak and hide food. She would even take money from her mother's purse so she could stop at McDonald's on the way home from school. As the binge episodes became more frantic, Virge felt guilty and remorseful after eating. She knew her mom and dad hated her fatness, but she didn't want to give up the one thing in life that made her feel good.

As Virge got bigger and bigger, her mom's suggestions that she diet intensified. Her mom always told her that she didn't care if Virge was fat and that she loved her anyway, but she knew Virge would feel better if she would lose a little weight. Virge could tell her mother was embarrassed about how fat her daughter was. She also knew her mother was just as embarrassed about her husband's drinking. Virge felt her mother's shame and became even more ashamed of herself.

Virge was fourteen at this time, and it was then that she began the diet cycle. Mom promised her if she lost 40 pounds she would give her one hundred dollars. As a matter of fact, Mom would go to a diet club with her and they could lose weight together. It would be fun.

Virge lost 30 pounds, and her mother was elated. People told both Virge and her mother how great Virge looked and what a pretty girl she was. Virge knew her mother wanted her to date, go to proms, and bring boyfriends home. Despite the praise, though, Virge recalled that she felt fearful and uncertain. She was scared to death of boys and didn't know what to do with them, but she never elaborated on this during our sessions. It was during this time in treatment that Virge began to skip appointments and talked about dropping out of treatment.

During this period of her life, when she was fourteen and had lost 30 pounds, Virge's dad, during one of his drinking episodes, approached her as she was studying in her bedroom. She recalled that Mom was doing laundry in the basement. Tearfully, she shared that he put his arms around her and kissed her. She said it wasn't the way a dad would kiss his daughter. He then began to fondle her breasts and told her how great she looked since she'd lost weight. She remembered being overwhelmed with shame and embarrassment. Then she felt angry, pushed him away, and told him to stay away from her. He cursed her and said she was a slut and no damn good.

After he left her room, Virge remembered crying and crying. She said at one point she looked in the mirror at herself and put her fist through it. She was terrified, horrified, and deeply ashamed. She wanted to tell her mother what had happened but also felt compelled to protect her mother. Fearing that her mother wouldn't listen or would misunderstand and that her father would deny it ever happened, Virge pretended nothing had ever happened. She swallowed her pain and turmoil and forced herself to forget what had happened.

Virge then began bingeing secretively again. She felt the need to please her mother by dieting, but her fear that her father would approach her again made the bingeing frantic. Virge felt her mother's disapproval every time she looked at her but the words were always, "I love you no matter how you look." Mom began to look for excuses as to why Virge was gaining weight, but she never asked Virge what was going on or how she felt. She took Virge to doctor after doctor, but Virge kept getting bigger. Nothing Mom tried seemed to work.

Virge plodded through adolescence feeling shameful and

inadequate. She made friends with a few other girls, but never really felt comfortable with boys. She was haunted by the thought that she might be a lesbian. As she moved into adulthood, she had a few lesbian relationships, but never found them very satisfying. She never felt as though she could connect with anyone. Not having anyone to talk to about her sexual concerns, Virge continued to think there was something wrong with her.

Until Virge entered treatment she didn't associate her inability to stay on a diet with her fear of losing weight. She always thought she wanted to lose weight and just didn't have what it took to succeed.

It wasn't until she recalled the episode with her father and shared her feelings about it that Virge began to look at her compulsive eating and the effects of growing up in an alcoholic family with more honesty.

As treatment progressed, Virge identified the rules of her alcoholic family and the role she played. She saw she had been taught to avoid conflict and to repress her thoughts and feelings. She understood why she felt overly responsible for others but was fearful of letting anyone get too close to her.

She realized she played both roles of the Banner Carrier and Clown while growing up, and she explored how she continued these roles in her adult relationships.

As Virge was more open and honest about herself and her feelings, she experienced less shame and was able to tolerate uncomfortable feelings. The intensity and frequency of her obsession with food and compulsive eating decreased. She had more intimate friendships and became more involved in O.A. meetings and with the people she met there. With time she was able to help others and was able to ask for and receive help from others.

At the end of therapy, Virge has developed a healthier system of living. She is losing weight slowly, but isn't having a "perfect" recovery. She has periodic relapses, especially during stress or conflict with others. But she's no longer so overwhelmed with guilt and shame that she isolates and eats herself into oblivion. Instead, she calls her sponsor and other friends, talks about her struggles in O.A. meetings, renews her commitment to her recovery program, and gets on with her life in a responsible and meaningful manner.

When I see Virge walking now, I see a woman in a healthy body who stands erect and who has a sense of dignity and self-respect.

Maggie's Story

After my first session with Maggie, I questioned why she was seeking therapy. She really seemed well put together: she was attractive, outgoing, had a good marriage, and an eighteen-year-old daughter (from a previous marriage) that she got along with quite well. She had a busy law practice, was involved in professional organizations, and had an enjoyable social life, both with her husband, married couples, and with her women friends. Her hobbies included skiing, reading, and mineral collecting.

After she shared this initial information with me, she was very direct in talking about her eating disorder. She had gone on a strict diet when she quit smoking (she had gained 30 pounds) and suddenly found herself bingeing. Although she didn't vomit or use laxatives, she exercised and dieted frantically. She became obsessed about not gaining her weight back.

She knew her diet drove her to bingeing, but she also knew there was more to it than that. As a teenager, she never had a weight problem. She was a tall, young girl with a large frame. On her dad's side of the family the women tended to be overweight. He often said he hoped she wouldn't take after them. Since she was so tall, she could gain weight without it being noticeable. She dieted on and off when in her twenties, but it wasn't as extreme.

When she started feeling out of control with food, she was frightened. She had read about eating disorders but never thought she could be a victim.

As therapy progressed, Maggie reported a deep sense of hopelessness. On most days, she felt blue and not happy with herself. In spite of her good relationship with her husband and daughter, and her successful practice, she still felt empty inside. She knew she had a great deal to be grateful for, yet she felt guilty for not being happy with what she saw as her blessings.

She had been married twice before (for which she felt a great deal of shame) and knew that she was not equipped to be a responsible partner in a committed relationship. When she met Chas, her current husband, she felt it was through his maturity and emotional health that she was able to have healthier relationships. She attributed the success of their marriage to his acceptance of her.

This issue of acceptance was a critical theme for Maggie. When we began to explore why it was so important to her, she talked about her birth family. Maggie was the youngest of three children. Her dad had his own business while her mother stayed home and took care of the children. Maggie's sister and mom were close, while she felt a special bond with her dad, particularly when she was little.

Her brother Joe was the favorite, although he was ten years older than she and she didn't remember his being around much. He was "like a visiting dignitary." When she was in junior high, he was away at college; he moved to another state when he graduated.

Her brother always seemed more important to her parents than she or her sister. They always talked about Joe's achievements, Joe's dates, or Joe's friends. Maggie also believed that Joe was wonderful. She idolized him and wanted to be just like him. All the excitement around the house always seemed to center around Joe.

As she talks about those times, she now realizes she felt inferior because she was a girl, just like her mother who was stuck at home with dirty laundry and dirty dishes.

The men seemed to be out in the world having a wonderful time. Her dad was always out with clients having dinner or traveling. Her mother wouldn't go on trips with him because she wouldn't leave the children with a babysitter. When Joe was home, her mother was in a better mood, fixed Joe special meals, and hovered about him making sure he was taken care of.

Being female meant nothing more than waiting on men. Maggie remembered being jealous of her brother for all this attention, but guilt would soon overcome her. After all, Joe deserved all of it; he was wonderful.

Her bond with her dad was a way to have some of his qualities rub off on her, a way to be close to her brother. Her dad idolized Joe. She would tag along with her dad, and he would always brag about Joe wherever they went. Maggie remembers feeling an ache inside when she would hear about Joe, when she would see her dad's face light up as he talked about Joe. She wanted to make her dad feel as good about her as Joe. So she thought she would be just like Joe. She knew she didn't want to be like her sister or her mother; their lives seemed dull. She pulled away from her mother and her sister, seeing them as unimportant. Many times she felt rage toward them and would lash out. She knows now this rage was her own self-hate at being female.

As she moved into adolescence, Maggie's relationship with her dad changed. She noticed he didn't have as much time for her and he wasn't as affectionate with her; he seemed to distance himself from her. Now she thinks back and sees that he had difficulty with his little girl's changing body. But at the time, she felt rejected and hurt. Without his love, she felt alone since she had alienated herself from her mother and sister.

When Joe was twenty (Maggie was ten), she remembers her mom and dad talking secretively, telling her to go off and play. She was always puzzled by these very private conversations.

After graduating from college, Joe moved to another state. Things then became even more secretive at home. Her parents would get phone calls and would tell her and her sister to leave the room. They would suddenly leave home and when Maggie or her sister would ask where they were going, they would say, "Where we go is none of your business."

Maggie doesn't remember when or how, but around the age of eighteen, she discovered her brother had a problem with alcohol and other drugs. This was the secret her parents had been hiding from the girls. She found out her parents sent Joe money to bail him out of what he described as financial problems. She learned the financial problems were to support his drug and drinking habit.

Her parents became preoccupied with protecting the family image of Joe as the family's symbol of success. When Maggie reflects on those days, she remembers feeling a deep sense of helplessness.

She and her sister were always good girls—cooperative, kind, and loving. She discovered she was beginning to have feelings she was ashamed of. She was beginning to hate Joe and her parents. Why did they continue to protect him? She remembers they were so preoccupied with Joe that she felt invisible.

Her older sister also tried to protect Joe. So Maggie never felt anyone at home was really interested in her.

In high school she felt lonely and isolated. Even though she had friends, they were temporary relationships. She floated through high school feeling lost. She became involved with boys and looked for one who would make her feel all right about herself. None of them did.

College was filled with turmoil for Maggie. Her relationship with her family became more strained and she felt more invisible. She desperately sought to find a connection somewhere. All of the men she dated were just like her brother. She now refers to his type as peacocks: all "flash and dash but no substance." These "glass connections" as she called them, "were based on fragile images; they all ended in pain."

When she was 25, she decided to make something of herself. She applied to law school, got accepted, and did extremely well. Her accomplishments were met by her parents with, "We are very proud of you," but as soon as the words were spoken they would express concern for Joe. This would enrage Maggie. She moved away and continued to achieve, trying to make up for the disappointment her parents felt with Joe. It was a way to distract them from what a mess he was and to see some value in her, but it never worked.

To this day, Maggie's parents are still protecting Joe and bailing him out of his financial and legal problems. Through therapy, Maggie sees she's a product of a codependent family system. She recognizes her role as the Invisible Child and is trying to break through the glass image in her relationships with others. She's working on building a self-image that isn't tied up in pleasing others. She's struggling with coming to terms with herself as a female and how she's split off this side of herself.

She's able to see her brother as sick and in need of treatment, but she doesn't feel the need to fix him or the family.

Since she's become aware of her codependency and her repressed feelings, she's less preoccupied with her weight. She regularly attends ACOA meetings and works the Twelve Steps most of the time.

Maggie now knows that chasing and protecting Joe's

image has been a way to ignore her self, a self that she's beginning to discover is worthwhile and lovable.

Nan's Story

Weighing 180 pounds at five-foot-two, Nan describes herself as a "fireplug." With her red hair, she thinks this is an accurate description of herself. Even though there's a smile on her face when she starts to say it, her eyes look to the floor by the time it's out of her mouth.

Nan was in her 40s when she sought treatment for her eating disorder. A compulsive eater struggling with weight, she tried many times to lose weight, including buying almost every diet book on the market. Her bookshelves at home were loaded with books promising to make her thin. When she got tired of reading, she would go to diet clubs, and when she got tired of being weighed in and hearing personal stories of miraculous weight loss, she would start eating all over again. By the time she entered therapy for compulsive eating, she felt like a total failure.

In group therapy, Nan presented herself as likable, self-reliant, and responsible, whose only real problem in life was being too heavy. She said if she could get the weight off and keep it off, her life would be happy.

As treatment progressed, Nan listened to the other group members, offering them feedback and support. She appeared reluctant to share her story, but began to talk more about the problems she was having at home with her husband and children.

It wasn't until a group session focused on relationships with mothers and fathers that Nan became agitated. She became angry and talked about how controlling her mother was and how difficult it was to cope with her. As the group asked more questions, it became apparent that, although Nan felt controlled by her mother, she also felt responsible for her. She would call and talk with her mother almost daily and had her over for dinner almost every weekend.

Perplexed by this double message, the group asked Nan to share more about her childhood. Then the family secret regarding Nan's father's "drinking problem" began to surface.

Nan was the middle child and only girl, with one brother two years older and the other brother five years younger than she. Her parents remained married and living together until her father's death when Nan was 40.

Her father never entered treatment or a recovery program for his alcoholism. Nan shared that she didn't remember her father not being alcoholic. She remembers little of her preschool life, except for a feeling of being secure and comfortable with her mother. She has no memory of her relationship with her father during those years, although she has been told by her mother that she was very close to her father.

She remembers that once she started hearing schoolmates talk about their families, she became aware that what she had always assumed was natural and normal was not. Prior to this time, she remembers her parents arguing but didn't connect the arguments with drinking.

When Nan was in the sixth grade, her dad's drinking began to get worse. Her family lived across the street from school. When he would go on his drinking binges, her father would often sleep it off in the car, which was parked in front of the house. The other kids would make fun of her father who was "drunker than a skunk!"

As she shared this memory, sadness and anger welled up within her as she related the humiliation she experienced when this would happen. She would run across the street into the house and slam the door to her bedroom. There she would shake with anger and cry until dinnertime.

Even though her mother knew why she was so upset, her mother never talked with her about how she felt. Nan's mom would talk about everything else, asking Nan how school was or sharing what happened to her at home that day, but she never acknowledged her husband was passed out in the car. Mom went about her business and made dinner for Nan's brothers and her. Dad never ate with them. It was as if he was invisible.

As she started high school, he wouldn't come home at all. This got to be a particular problem on paydays. She remembers no one being concerned about her father but being very concerned about the money. Once she got old enough to drive, she or her older brother was often sent out by her mother to find her father and get his paycheck so he wouldn't spend it all on alcohol.

All through her adolescence, the emotional separation and lack of closeness created a deep chasm in Nan's relationship with her dad. She had experienced conflicting feelings that ranged from love to pity to rage.

Nan said she always felt her mother was the only parent. Through the earlier years, being with Mother made her feel safe and secure. But at age thirteen, she began to feel smothered by her. She felt her mother depended on her a great deal and that she always had to be there in case her mother needed her.

Many times she didn't go out on dates or to parties because she felt she had to be at home with her mother. She felt sorry for her, all alone. Her older brother left home and joined the service, and her younger brother was a loner, off in his room reading. Nan felt obligated to take care of her mother and to make up for her father and her brothers, who didn't seem to care much about Mom. Nan's mother repeatedly told her that she didn't know what she'd do without her. Although this initially made Nan feel good, later it became a burden.

She recalls being what her mom described as a "solidly

built" girl. Nan describes her family's attitude toward food and weight as unclear. Her mother expressed concern about Nan being "a little too solid," but she would always buy Nan's favorite foods. This always confused her, but it wouldn't last long as she munched potato chips and drank soda every day after school.

She remembers sneaking and hiding food when she was ten years old. Through therapy, she connected this memory with the shame she felt about her dad's drunkenness being seen by her classmates. When her mom wasn't looking, she'd grab cookies and take them to her bedroom. There she would binge while sobbing.

When her mom confronted her one day with dozens of empty candy bar wrappers and empty cookie bags, Nan felt a deep flush of shame and embarrassment. She broke down and cried and her mom told her she shouldn't feel bad; she just shouldn't be eating food in her bedroom. "After all, I don't want bugs up here." They never talked about this incident again.

Her compulsive eating continued, and she gained weight but would often diet and loose some of it. Her weight fluctuated throughout high school.

In spite of her eating, Nan was the perfect daughter. She made good grades, was valedictorian of her class, and got a scholarship to college. She was her mother's shining star. She always thought of her and her mother as close, inseparable. As a teenager and young adult, she was proud of their relationship. Most of her friends would complain about their mothers, but not Nan. Her mother was her best friend.

Nan would tell her mother everything, and her mother would do the same. Her mom would complain about Nan's dad and his drinking and would seek Nan's advice on how to handle it. In spite of this special bond she felt they shared, there was a deep feeling inside that this wasn't right.

As she became closer to her mother, she felt more alienated from her father. She found it difficult to look at him because she felt such contempt for him. On days when he wasn't drinking, she felt pity for him; he looked so disheveled and lost.

This relationship with Mom continued until Nan became serious with Steve, whom she eventually married. Nan's mother had difficulty letting go of Nan, her "Rock of Gibraltar," and saw Steve as a threat to their relationship.

Nan's weight stopped fluctuating once she married Steve. She had lost a great deal of weight right before the wedding so she could get into a size nine wedding dress. After their first child was born, Nan's weight began to increase and continued to be high.

Nan felt torn between her mother and Steve. They both complained about the other. After a few years of marriage, Nan repeated the triangular relationship she had as a youngster at home, only this time the person on the outside was Steve. She found her mom continually criticizing him, much like she did Nan's dad. This entanglement with her mother became more intense when Nan's dad died. Nan's mother demanded more and more of her time. She expected Nan to call and visit her daily. Her mom would give Nan negative messages about Steve and tell her he didn't appreciate her. After trying to understand her mother's viewpoint, anger would begin to well up within Nan. She would defend Steve, not because she disagreed with her mother, but because she felt rage toward her mother for having to defend herself for choosing Steve as a husband. These explosive episodes were followed with overwhelming feelings of guilt when she would go home and binge.

Not only did she have to defend herself to her mother, but to Steve as well. He would also express his anger at how controlling and dominating her mother was and felt Nan's mother was more important to her than he was.

Once again, Nan tried to understand Steve's feelings, but the anger would surge. Nan would then defend her relationship with her mother, not because she disagreed with him, but because something inside of her felt a need to defend herself. These episodes would also end in bingeing. Nan felt split in two, always trying to understand everyone else's feelings but her own.

Through treatment, Nan identified herself as the Banner Carrier. She interacted with others with a sense of "I've got to be the fixer—take on responsibility for everyone and make everything right."

She has come to terms with how her compulsive eating is an addictive illness. She realizes her bingeing is a way to numb the painful feelings she felt toward her dad. Through therapy she has gotten in touch with the full range of feelings she had toward her dad—the loving, warm feelings as well as the hurt and anger. She realizes her out of control eating was a way to identify with and be close to her dad, who was out of control with his drinking. No matter what her mother did to alienate Nan from her dad, Nan now knows their addictions were the only things beyond her mother's grasp.

In recovery, Nan sees herself as searching for an identity beyond her role of Banner Carrier. She has taken steps to detach from her mother and is developing a give-and-take relationship with Steve.

Nan is also detaching from her role as intermediary between her husband and her mother. Although it sometimes requires her to "bite my tongue or leave the house for a while," Nan often lets her husband and her mother settle their own quarrels. She refuses to get in the middle when either of them has a complaint about the other. She's working hard to be more assertive and open, and she is encouraging her family to do the same.

THE TWELVE STEPS OF O.A.

1. We admitted we were powerless over food—that our lives had become unmanageable.

2. Came to believe that a Power greater than ourselves could restore us to sanity.

3. Made a decision to turn our will and our lives over to the care of God *as we understood Him.*

4. Made a searching and fearless moral inventory of ourselves.

5. Admitted to God, to ourselves, and to another human being the exact nature of our wrongs.

6. Were entirely ready to have God remove all these defects of character.

7. Humbly asked Him to remove our shortcomings.

8. Made a list of all persons we had harmed, and became willing to make amends to them all.

9. Made direct amends to such people wherever possible, except when to do so would injure them or others.

10. Continued to take personal inventory and when we were wrong promptly admitted it.

11. Sought through prayer and meditation to improve our conscious contact with God *as we understood Him,* praying only for knowledge of His will for us and the power to carry that out.

12. Having had a spiritual awakening as the result of these steps, we tried to carry this message to compulsive overeaters and to practice these principles in all our affairs.*

---

*Adapted from the Twelve Steps of Alcoholics Anonymous, reprinted with permission of A.A. World Services, Inc., New York, N.Y.

SOURCES OF HELP

Adult Children of Alcoholics, 31706 Coast Highway,
Number 201, South Laguna, CA 92677 (714) 499-3889.

Al-Anon Family Group Headquarters, Inc., P.O. Box 862,
Midtown Station, New York, NY 10018-0862 (212) 302-7240.

American Anorexia/Bulimia Association, 133 Cedar Lane,
Teaneck, NJ 07666 (201) 836-1800.

ANAD-National Association of Anorexia Nervosa &
Associated Disorders, P.O. Box 7, Highland Park, IL 60035
(312) 831-3438.

ANRED-Anorexia Nervosa/Related Eating Disorders, P.O.
Box 5102, Eugene, OR 97405 (503) 344-1144.

Center for the Study of Anorexia and Bulimia, 1 West 91st
Street, New York, NY 10024 (212) 595-3449.

National Anorexic Aid Society, 5796 Karl Road, Columbus,
OH 43229 (614) 436-1112.

SUGGESTED READING

Boskind-White, Marlene, and William C. White. *Bulimarexia: The Binge-Purge Cycle.* New York: W. W. Norton and Co., Inc., 1983.

Bruch, Hilde. *Eating Disorders: Obesity, Anorexia Nervosa, and the Person Within.* New York: Basic Books, Inc., 1973.

Bruch, Hilde. *The Golden Cage: The Enigma of Anorexia Nervosa.* New York: Harvard University Press, 1978.

Chernin, Kim. *The Obsession: Reflections on the Tyranny of Slenderness.* New York: Harper & Row, 1981

Chernin, Kim. *The Hungry Self: Women, Eating and Identity.* New York: Harper & Row, 1985.

Crisp, A. H. *Anorexia Nervosa: Let Me Be.* New York: Grune & Stratton, 1980.

Hollis, Judi. *Fat Is a Family Affair.* Center City, Minn.: Hazelden Educational Materials, 1985.

Hollis, Judi. *Hope For Compulsive Eaters Workbook.* Center City, Minn.: Hazelden Educational Materials, 1986.

Levenkron, Steven. *The Best Little Girl in the World.* New York: Warner Books, Inc., 1978.

McFarland, Barbara, and Tyeis Baker-Baumann. *Sexuality and Compulsive Eating.* Center City, Minn.: Hazelden Educational Materials, 1987

McFarland, Barbara, and Rodney Susong. *Killing Ourselves With Kindness.* Center City, Minn.: Hazelden Educational Materials, 1985.

Orbach, Susie. *Fat Is a Feminist Issue.* London: Berkley Publishing Group, 1978.

——. *Fat Is a Feminist Issue II.* London: Berkley Publishing Group, 1982.

SELECT BIBLIOGRAPHY

Ackerman, Robert J. *Children of Alcoholics*. Holmes Beach, Fla.: Learning Publications, Inc., 1979.

Bepko, Claudia. *The Responsibility Trap*. New York: The Free Press, 1985.

Root, Maria P. et al. *Bulimia: A Systems Approach To Treatment*. New York: Penguin Books, 1986.

Wegscheider-Cruse, Sharon. *Another Chance*. Palo Alto, Calif.: Science and Behavior Books, Inc., 1981.

Woititz, Janet Geringer. *Adult Children of Alcoholics*. Pompano Beach, Fla.: Health Communications, Inc., 1983.

Woititz, Janet Geringer. *Struggle for Intimacy*. Pompano Beach, Fla.: Health Communications, Inc.

INDEX